MASTERCLASS

The Biography of

George Headley

by

Bridgette Lawrence

Published by
POLAR PUBLISHING (UK) LTD

Dedication
To all those who helped compile this tribute to one of cricket's unsung heroes:
Michael Arnold, John Barnes, Julian Baskcomb, Paul Bateman, Sir Donald Bradman,
Yvonne Chew, Harvey Depass, Errol Edwards, Ray Goble, Ron Headley, Sheila
Lawrence, Roger Mann, David Reynolds, Reg Scarlett, Gordon Smith, Harry Thomas,
Sylvia Thomas, Gordon Vidler and Noel White.

First published in Great Britain by
Polar Publishing (UK) Ltd
2, Uxbridge Road, Leicester LE4 7ST
England.

ISBN 1 899538 05 4

Designed and printed by
Polar Print Group Ltd,
2, Uxbridge Road, Leicester, England.
Telephone: 0116 261 0800

Photographs are courtesy of
The Roger Mann Collection, Colorsport, Hulton-Deutsch, Sports-Line Photographic

Contents

Foreword
by Sir Donald Bradman AC 4

Introduction 5

Chapter 1
A Latin Life 7

Chapter 2
Taming a Lord 11

Chapter 3
Testing Times 17

Chapter 4
An Australian Baptism 27

Chapter 5
1932: A World Record Year 39

Chapter 6
West Indies Expect 47

Chapter 7
Lancashire Hot Pot 53

Chapter 8
A Triumphant Homecoming 57

Chapter 9
Immortal at Lord's 61

Chapter 10
A Waiting Game 69

Chapter 11
Indian Summer 81

Chapter 12
A Professional Calling 85

Chapter 13
Dudley Days 91

Chapter 14
Coach and Mentor 93

Chapter 15
Is that George Headley? 105

Chapter 16
Close of Play 115

Career Record 121

Foreword

by Sir Donald Bradman AC

The first tour of Australia by a West Indian cricket team was in 1930-31 when I had the pleasure of meeting with and playing against George Headley.

Although George had previously exhibited his prowess at home he had not done so overseas. But we saw enough of him that season to realise another bright star was on the horizon.

This promise was fulfilled to the extent that in nominating him as one of the five cricketers of the year in 1933, the editor of *Wisden* referred to him as "beyond all question the best batsman the West Indies have ever produced".

Since then of course the West Indies have bred an astonishing array of marvellous batsmen, Weekes, Worrell, Walcott, Sobers, Kallicharran, Richards and others. Some of Headley's admirers still think he was the best of them all and statistics lend support to such a view.

Amongst all those who played 20 or more Test innings his average ranks third to me and R G Pollock, a mere .14 behind second place, and he only misses third place behind me and V M Merchant in *Wisden's* first-class career averages because he is 79 short of their 10,000 run qualification.

Clarrie Grimmett, the finest of all slow leg-spinners (I put O'Reilly in another category) who was probably around his peak in 1930, said that George Headley played him better than anyone else - a wonderful compliment.

What impressed me most was the lateness with which he played his shots and his strength off the back foot.

I could go on at great length about his batting prowess and achievements, but the figures speak for themselves. What they don't reveal is the charm and personality of the man behind them. It was in this field that George set such a wonderful example. In assessing the greatness of any athlete I place immense store on modesty and George had this quality in full measure.

After his Australian tour we corresponded with one another and the depth of his thinking, his sense of fairness and understanding, always shone through his letters.

Subsequently it was my good fortune to meet and establish friendships with many other West Indians, men like Frank Worrell and Jeff Stollmeyer, who did so much to uplift the status of the West Indies on the world cricket scene, but to me George Headley will always remain a special memory because he was the pioneer who blazed the trail.

I give thanks for the life of a truly great sportsman and gentleman.

4

Introduction

THIS long overdue biography looks at the life of one of cricket's unsung heroes, the Jamaican and West Indian Test player, George Alphonso Headley. Don Bradman apart, Headley was almost certainly the finest batsman of his generation, yet by comparison with "The Don" relatively little has been written about him.

Hopefully this book goes a long way towards rectifying this situation by giving an insight into an outstanding cricketer and remarkable man: the way in which he coped with the pressures of being an outstanding black sportsman obliged to compete within a stultifying colonial environment, but nonetheless rose through the ranks to become their first black Test captain.

It traces Headley triumphs from when he scored a century on his Test debut against England in 1930 to when he became the first West Indian to score a Test hundred in Australia the following year, his 344 in a world record partnership against Lord Tennyson's touring team in Jamaica in 1932 and, his finest hour, when he became the first man to score two centuries in a Test at Lord's, in 1939.

There were the low points too: notably his brushes with authority, mostly as he sought to improve the welfare of fellow players; and the intense disappointment he felt at being passed over for the West Indies captaincy for so long.

Headley's achievements are remarkable in their own right, but seem even more noteworthy when one considers that, unlike Bradman, he could never depend on his batting partners for support. This is illustrated by the fact that in 15 out of 35 Test innings he played for the West Indies he was the top-scorer, in 11 of those he made at least a third of the runs and in three it was more than half the total.

Beside his great deeds on the field of play, the generous personality of the so-called "Atlas" of West Indian cricket is captured time and again with anecdotes from some of his contemporaries whose stories illustrate not only his insatiable appetite for cricket but, also, for life.

Bridgette Lawrence
London, 1995

CHAPTER ONE

A LATIN LIFE

GEORGE ALPHONSO HEADLEY is a cricketing legend. Without doubt one of the finest batsmen ever to emerge from the Caribbean - many would argue the finest of all-time, and that debate could fill a book in its own right - Headley was unique in that he had to cope with two difficulties that did not affect his English and Australian counterparts. Namely shouldering his team's batting almost alone and, secondly, handling the social iniquities and blind prejudice that were an inherent facet of West Indian life in colonial times.

George Headley was born in Colon, Panama on 30 May 1909 after his father had gone there to help build the Panama Canal. The first son of Irene Roberts, from Jamaica, and DeCourcy Headley, from Barbados, his parents had been attracted overseas by the better wages offered by the Americans who were building the waterway to link the Caribbean Sea to the Pacific Ocean.

The heavy American influence meant that in Panama they played baseball, not cricket, and George quickly developed such a panache for the game that all the local youngsters wanted him in their team. He learned all sorts of techniques in baseball that were to stand him in good stead in his later sporting life, such as pulling his hands back as the ball entered his grasp so as to soften its impact.

By the time George was five years old work on the Canal had finished and his father went to Cuba in search of employment. At the age of 10 George was taken to Jamaica by his mother. She was concerned that her son was speaking more Spanish than English and felt that it would benefit him to attend an English-speaking school in Jamaica. But the South American influence never left him entirely, and as he got older he cut a debonair figure with his matching ties and socks.

George enjoyed an idyllic youth in Jamaica, even if the sea-crossing made him ill and meant that he arrived on the island in poor shape. The youngster lived with Irene's sister-in-law, Mrs Roberts, in Rae Town, a district in Kingston. He was soon being spoiled as the 'baby' of the family, as his aunt had two grown-up daughters of her own and a son, Cyril, in his late teens. Irene Headley joined her husband in Cuba, but throughout her life corresponded regularly with George.

As in Panama, life revolved around school, church and sport (although not necessarily in that order) for George. He had attended the Anglican church with his

❏ *One of the earliest photographs of the young George Headley in cricketing attire.*

mother and was a soloist in the choir, but in Kingston they were Methodists and he went to Sunday school and morning and evening services with the rest of his 'new' family. In his teens, he joined the Church Lads' Brigade at St George's Methodist Church but later returned to the Anglican church, attending St Michael's. Religion always played an important part in George's life and he often put his success down to "a little prayer and a little luck".

If his religious orientation changed when he arrived in Kingston, so did his sporting one, and it was in Rae Town that he learned to play cricket. The gear was makeshift, but what they lacked in equipment the local youngsters made up for in ingenuity: bats were made from fallen coconut boughs and young breadfruits or pebbles firmly encased in cloth served as balls; pads and gloves, needless to say, were not even thought of.

When not playing cricket, George toned himself up by swimming, usually between Kingston Harbour from the Paradise Street beach to Palisadoes and back again, a total of about three miles. He and his friends would spend time at a place they called 'High Bush' before making their return journey. When he first arrived in Jamaica, George had not been able to swim, but taught himself by floating on a piece of bamboo and propelled himself along with his hands until he was confident enough to dispense with the float. He loved the sea and would often spend all night fishing, which was one of his favourite relaxations.

He attended Calabar Elementary School where the headmaster, H A Stephenson, ran a cricket club with an entrance fee of three pence and a penny a week. The idea was that the money could be used to buy kit; even so, the budget didn't extend to wicket-keeping gloves, so that position usually fell to George who could be relied upon to take the ball without them. Many of the other youngsters put it down to his 'iron hands', but the truth lay in his knack of gathering the ball without injuring himself in the way he had learnt while playing baseball, together with his remarkably early sighting of the ball.

C L R James recalled in *Beyond a Boundary* how George had told him that from the time he began to play cricket he saw every ball bowled come out of the bowler's hand, and added that if he did not see it out of the bowler's hand he would be at a loss how to play.

In Rae Town they used to play a game called 'catch-ball-bowl' after school until it was too dark to see. But then George started to spoil the fun: he went in to bat one Monday afternoon, and continued through Tuesday, Wednesday and Thursday afternoons. He should not have been surprised when no one turned up on Friday although, given his professional approach even in those days, he was somewhat disappointed.

After Calabar, George attended Kingston High School, which later became St John's College. There, the Principal was not such a keen sports fan but still allowed his pupils away from school early to practise at nearby Clovelly Park. However, the real improvement in George's game came when he had the opportunity to take part in all-day Saturday matches at Crabhole Park, near the Bellevue area of Kingston. The Park earned its peculiar name because crabs made their homes in holes they had dug in the sandy soil there; whatever the boys were using for balls would often drop into these holes and they would have to get water from the sea to float them to the surface.

The youngsters were so enthusiastic that they made their own wickets at Crabhole with clay from the nearby grounds of a hospital close to Doncaster and Paradise Streets. Although, to them, it was just a practical consideration given the nature of the park, it meant that they became used to playing on a proper surface at an earlier age than most. Indeed, the group of boys he played with began to win something of a reputation, with George's ability in particular arousing local interest. Dr J J Cameron, who worked at the local hospital and had two sons who went on to play for Jamaica and West Indies, invited them to play at the hospital on Wednesdays and Thursdays. Then, on Saturdays, the British Regiment at Port Royal would send a boat over to collect the boys. These were enjoyable occasions - with George usually scoring most of the runs - and made even more popular by the lavish 'teas'!

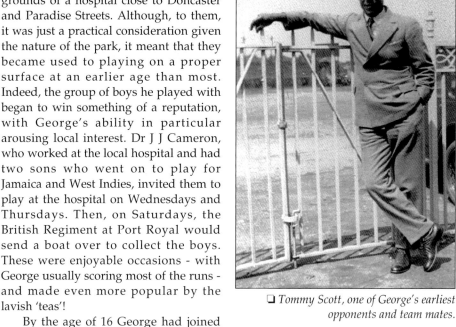

❑ *Tommy Scott, one of George's earliest opponents and team mates.*

By the age of 16 George had joined Raeton Cricket Club, which attracted young players from the Rae Town and Brown's Town districts. On one occasion, Raeton had a fixture against Stony Hill Approved School, who were captained by Tommy Scott, Jamaica's gifted slow bowler who was to become one of West Indies' first Test players. Their ground was above Constant Spring, north of Kingston, and the school usually sent down a horse-drawn wagon to collect players for such matches but, on that occasion, George and Wellesley Alexander missed the wagon. Determined to take part in the fixture, the pair walked several miles to the ground and still arrived in time for the start.

However, George was something of a loner. Throughout his life he chose his friends carefully and tended to avoid much of the bonhomie that gripped some of his more carefree colleagues. He was always content to sit and watch the game and when it was his turn to field or bat he would concentrate tirelessly on the job in hand. It has been said of others with less justification, but George really did live for batting. C L R James commented on his powers of concentration much later on: "Once he starts to walk down the pavilion steps he would not be able to recognise his own father if he met him half-way. Everything is out of his mind except batting."

In 1925 George scored his first century in a formal cricket setting, for Raeton CC in a friendly match against Clovelly at the large Clovelly Park ground. Coming in at number three, he scored 105 and made the position his own.

CHAPTER TWO
TAMING A LORD

G EORGE had his first taste of first-class cricket in 1921 when his cousin, Cyril, invited him to watch the play-off between two local clubs, Melbourne and Lucas, who were tied on points. In the event, they did not have enough money for the entrance fee into Kensington Park and had to content themselves with viewing the match perched precariously on the branches of a guango tree. Not for the first time, the young Headley would watch and learn from the batting stars of the day who, on that occasion, included J K Holt Snr, Karl Nunes, Frank Martin and 'Kitty' Morales.

George's own entry into competitive cricket was made possible by his first job. With his appointment as temporary clerk at the Half-Way-Tree Magistrate's Court, he was able to play for the St Andrew's Police side in the Junior Cup competition although, like himself, not many of the side were actual police officers. In his first season he helped them to tie with St Catherine CC in the Cup, although his first-ball dismissal in the play-off condemned his side in much the same way that other teams would struggle, notably the West Indies, when he was dismissed cheaply.

Despite his disappointing showing in that match, his earlier performances brought an invitation to attend the practice sessions with the Jamaica Colts team in 1926. But it wasn't easy for the young Headley to attend, as he didn't finish work at the court until four o'clock in the afternoon when the net sessions began. (Incidentally, many of the youngsters who played for the Colts came from more affluent families than George, and earning a living was less of a priority.) Because his place of work was some distance outside Kingston he could not get there on time and therefore could not be considered for the matches against the touring English side, led by Lord Tennyson, in 1927.

Always a stoic, Headley made the best of a trying situation and had to content himself with admiring Ernest Tyldesley's batting technique, as the Englishman scored three hundreds against Jamaica. He watched him intently as Tyldesley's excellent timing allowed him to score runs all round the wicket, and absorbed what he had learned into his considerable cricketing brain. George was particularly impressed with Tyldesley's control when he batted at Melbourne Park after the rain had fallen, and arguably learned as much from the boundary as if he had played.

❑ *Ernest Tyldesley, whose batting technique was admired by the young Headley.*

Later in 1927 Headley changed jobs and began work at the Keeling-Lindo Estates in St Catherine, which meant higher pay and closer proximity to Kingston. He joined St Catherine CC, who were captained by his new boss, Leonard Caryll, and also included W G Beckford and Tommy Scott. Because of his firm's enthusiasm for cricket, employees were allowed time off to practise and play matches. During his first season with St Catherine Headley helped them to win both the Junior and Senior Cups, and he was able to attend the Jamaican nets regularly. To earn extra money, Headley also worked for the Jamaica Fruit and Shipping Company and was fortunate that the boss there was also a cricket enthusiast, and former member of the St Catherine team, which meant he could combine his work and cricketing careers relatively easily, even if it did mean very little sleep.

At that time however the young Headley had no thoughts of making a life in cricket. Indeed, a brief period without work had made him contemplate a career in dentistry in America. But then fate intervened: the late arrival of his papers from Panama to apply for a US work permit allowed the young Headley to make his first-class debut for Jamaica, against Lord Tennyson's side who were touring again.

Tennyson, who played for Hampshire and had once captained England, was a popular figure and his teams often included cricketing stars such as Wally Hammond, Phil Mead, Percy Chapman, Percy Holmes, Andy Sandham, Maurice Allom, Percy Fender, Ewart Astill, 'Nobby' Clark, Morris Nichols and Greville Stevens.

Because Jamaica was geographically isolated from the rest of the cricket-playing islands in the Caribbean, these visits by English touring teams played an important part in the development of the game there and, indeed, in the development of George's reputation. Many years later Frank Worrell observed in a brief résumé of Jamaican cricket: "Even in the 1920's when Jamaican cricket first came to be taken seriously, there were no heroes of the stature of Trinidad's St Hill, Learie Constantine, Piggy Piggott, or George John, nor Barbados' Challenor, Tarilton, Francis and Griffith nor Guyana's Snuffy Browne - J K Holt Senior and R K Nunes were only standard bearers for the men to come - such men as the incomparable George Headley."

In the first match against the Lord's team at Sabina Park, the home captain, Karl Nunes, won the toss and elected to bat. Headley prepared to go in at number three and, as so often, did not have long to wait. The first wicket fell with just 12 runs on the board whereupon the 'bow-legged, bright-eyed' Headley made his way to the wicket amidst enthusiastic applause. There were several reasons for the excitement of the crowd: he had won a place in their hearts after his showing in the Senior Cup but, perhaps, more than that they were willing the youngster, who did not come from a privileged background, to excel against the English aristocracy.

He appeared to have a shaky start facing up to Allom (who would soon take four Test wickets in five balls against New Zealand), dropping his bat the first time he made contact with the ball. It transpired that slippery footwear had caused the incident, and he settled immediately afterwards to cut the next ball for four. He then took eight runs from the next three balls and another four off fast bowler, Clark, lifted him to 16. But a change of bowler brought the tourists more success, as the young prodigy was caught out by the Lord off the bowling of Trevor Arnott.

When Headley came out for his second innings the crowd was more subdued, presumably anxious that this time there were only five runs on the board and their local hero was under even more pressure. But they needn't have worried, as he went for his shots from the start. The same type of ball that had accounted for him in the first innings was dispatched to the boundary, as was a bouncer from Clark that took him to 50 in even time. Indeed, his fluent cutting, pulling, driving and hooking prompted some of the crowd to christen him "J K Junior", after the famous John Holt Senior. (The latter did in fact have a son, John Holt Junior, who went on to play Test cricket for the West Indies.) In the end, George was dismissed for 71, making the Lord and his team realise they were facing genuine first-class opposition. Although other Jamaican batsmen, notably Nunes and Frank Martin, had made large scores against the Lord's team on previous occasions, Tennyson realised that George's batting was something extra special.

Predictably George was unhappy at being dismissed before reaching his century, but was quick to put things right in the second match at Melbourne Park. Tennyson's team batted first and scored 252. Late on the first afternoon Headley found himself in the middle with Jamaica's score on 12 for one. He began confidently and was unbeaten overnight on 22 out of a total of 39; the break gave him the opportunity to prepare mentally to play a big innings. On the resumption, he was more cautious in his approach until he reached his 50; then he opened up and went after the English bowlers, as a series of boundaries rocketed from his bat. He made 100 out of 188 and then went into overdrive as he crashed Hilder for four successive boundaries before turning on the Lord himself, who was punished for three consecutive fours on two occasions during the innings as, at one stage, Headley hit 13 fours in a row.

He was finally dismissed for 211, out of a total of 609, and was heard to remark nonchalantly: "I found myself timing the ball well, and when a player is doing that it follows as sure as night follows day that he will make runs." Tennyson, who had caught him out, was more fulsome in his praise, commenting: "I have seen [Charles] Macartney and [Victor] Trumper bat, but I do not think that when they were as old as George Headley they could have been better." This was a remarkable compliment given that Macartney was one of the most stylish batsmen to grace the game and Trumper was Australia's finest stroke-maker before the emergence of Don Bradman.

Altogether Headley made 409 runs in that series for an average of 81.80, prompting all thoughts of becoming a dentist to fade: now he would concentrate on loose, and not-so-loose, balls rather than loose teeth.

Indeed he had been so impressive that many people thought he would be an automatic choice for the inaugural Test series between England and West Indies, to be played in England in 1928. But he was not chosen, apparently because he was 'too young'. Instead the selectors put their faith in a number of players approaching their forties, although West Indies' supporters doubtless wished more progressive thinking had prevailed as news of their team's performances in the Tests filtered back to the Caribbean.

❏ *Lord Tennyson, who was mesmerised by the remarkable performances of the young Jamaican protégé against his touring English side.*

But Headley took the set-back in his stride and had an even more profitable season for St Catherine in the Senior Cup. When the season was over, he kept himself fit by swimming and playing table tennis. He wanted to be in top-class form for the start of the new season because Sir Julien Cahn's English team, that included Lord Tennyson, was due in the West Indies early in 1929.

Jamaica's first game against the English tourists was played on a wet wicket. Nunes and Ivan Barrow opened the innings for Jamaica, but a first ball duck for Nunes meant Headley was obliged to virtually open the innings. He knew the priority was to stay at the wicket to give the sun a chance to dry it out before the other batsmen came in. He and Barrow batted ˋcircumspectly through the morning session and were both dismissed shortly after lunch, with George having scored 44. But they had done an admirable job and set the scene for the later batsmen to capitalise on their good work: John Holt Snr and Ernest Rae made no mistake as they both scored centuries to help Jamaica to a total of over 400.

Soon after Headley was to gain a reputation as the best bad wicket player in the world and would have remembered many of the techniques of Ernest Tyldesley, whom he had observed so closely some years before. He explained his philosophy: "From early youth I welcomed a challenge in any phase of the game of cricket. I regarded a wicket that was wet or impaired as a challenge to my capabilities and skill. I wanted to see whether I could still dictate to the bowlers as I could on a perfect wicket. I was obliged to exercise more careful judgement as to when to hit or defend, and I had to improvise strokes since the ball left

❏ *The famous batting stance that was to bring despair to bowlers across the world.*

the pitch most awkwardly at times. However, it was in such circumstances that I proved that I was a versatile batsman."

By that time, there was no doubt in Jamaican minds that Headley was a versatile batsman and almost certainly the best one they had. The Jamaican Board confirmed that view when they invited him to join an Invitation XI to play the English visitors that included players from the other West Indian islands, notably Learie Constantine and Joe Small from Trinidad and George Francis from Barbados, who had all taken part in the Test series in England. The whole occasion caused great excitement in Jamaica, whose distance from the Eastern Caribbean meant they were excluded from most of the inter-island competition. Constantine attracted particular attention, and George himself enjoyed talking to the Trinidadian, whose famed enthusiasm for the game infected everyone who met him. George was also impressed by the speed the top fast bowlers were now engendering and realised he would have to adapt his game to cope with the new generation of pace men.

In the Invitation match he coped well enough with the bowlers, enhancing his reputation with a splendid 143, which helped the home side to victory and Headley to an average of over 50. Interestingly, although Constantine felt that George was a natural batsman who hit the ball very hard, he believed his strokes lacked polish. The fact that Constantine had revised his opinion by the time of the first Test in the Caribbean, in Barbados in January 1930, is indicative of the speed with which Headley modified and improved his game: each cricketing experience brought new information that was incorporated into his armoury. As C L R James put it: "Great batsmen are the same, they are not like you or me. An experience is automatically registered and henceforth functions as a permanent part of the organism."

During the 1928-29 season the Keeling-Lindo estates became the property of the United Fruit Company, who had offices in Kingston. That meant it was more convenient for George to play for Lucas CC rather than St Catherine, and also gave him the opportunity to practise more regularly. Lucas was captained by John Holt Snr and had also attracted Headley's Rae Town colleagues, Wellesley Alexander and George Townsend, to its ranks; Ken Weekes and Leslie Hylton, who were to become stars of the future, also played for Lucas.

In the late summer of 1929 Headley made his first tour abroad when he went to New York to play some exhibition matches against the Jamaican Athletic Club, which had been formed by Jamaicans living in the United States to raise the profile of cricket in the area. Headley also took the opportunity to visit his parents, who were living in America. He had not seen them for over 10 years and by then had two younger brothers he had never met. His family attended some of the matches that were highly competitive occasions, as the expatriate West Indians rekindled their fervour for the game: indeed, the match between a Jamaican XI and a Barbadian XI was one of the keenest contests!

CHAPTER THREE

TESTING TIMES

E ARLY in 1930 England arrived in the Caribbean to play the first official Test series. It was a decidedly under-strength squad, as the MCC also had a team in New Zealand at the same time, but there were some famous names about to bow out of the international arena in the tour party, and some less well-known ones who would go on to win recognition.

George was somewhere between the two: he was not yet an established figure in world cricket, but certainly a man with an enviable reputation. And, this time, there was no doubt that he would make his Test debut, even though he lived in Jamaica, the most northerly island, a factor that would have prejudiced the chances of lesser mortals. None of the Jamaicans who toured England in 1928 had distinguished themselves and, because of the financial restraints of the time, players from the island staging the Test match had a much better chance of being selected. In each of the four Tests of the 1930 series, the captain was chosen from the host island and only Headley's skills were deemed sufficiently indispensable for him to be selected for every match.

When the call came Headley travelled to Barbados on an 'Elders and Fyffes' boat and was met in Bridgetown by the Secretary of the West Indies Board of Control. It was an emotional experience for him as his father was Barbadian and he had heard so much about the famous Kensington Oval. He was taken to the Hotel Savoy where he met his room-mate, who turned out to be none other than the great Learie Constantine himself.

As he practised in the nets for the match, Headley was confident that only injury or illness could prevent him from making his Test debut; watching the two matches Barbados played against the tourists did nothing to alter his view. He was therefore somewhat taken aback when on the final afternoon of practice three selectors, Harold Austin, who had captained West Indies in England in 1923, George Challenor, the so-called 'father of West Indian batting' and Tim Tarilton, positioned themselves behind the nets just as he was about to take guard. He was then obliged to play against the new-ball bowling of Constantine, Herman Griffith and George Francis who were recognised as the most testing bowlers in the West Indies at that time. Headley applied himself with an almost resigned indignation, middling virtually everything

❏ Learie Constantine, who offered the young Headley sound advice on his Test debut.

that was bowled to him. At the end of the session, the three spectators left without comment and the young Headley had to buy a newspaper the following morning to confirm he was in the side.

It would have been an act of folly to have omitted him from the line-up, and his name duly appeared. Constantine was the first to congratulate him and had sound words of advice: "Play within your capabilities," he said, "it's just another game." The great day arrived, 11 January 1930, and West Indies' openers, Clifford Roach and Teddy Hoad, took guard. The flamboyant Roach was in top form, but Hoad, the white captain for the match, was not so commanding. Even so, the openers put on 90 for the first wicket, before Hoad was caught out for 24. Headley arrived in the middle and decided to go for his shots from the start; he made 21 confident runs before misjudging a slower ball from Jack O'Connor and was bowled. The partisan Bajan crowd were not impressed, and shouted the names of other local players who could have played in his place when he returned to the pavilion.

But, by the end of West Indies' second innings, the spectators had changed their minds and their chants. He scored a superb 176, becoming the first West Indian player to score a century on his Test debut and the second, after Roach, to reach three figures in a Test match, as he shared in stands of 156 with Roach and 142 with Frank de Caires. Between them they had the Englishmen running the full length and breadth of Kensington Oval and, when he was finally out, West Indies' latest centurion heard a different shout from the crowd, "That boy's not a Jamaican. He comes from the Headley's from down Bay Road." The writer in the Barbados *Advocate* was somewhat more accurate in his assessment when, in summing up the drawn match, he wrote: "Of the batsmen I place Headley in the premier position. He is a first-class batsman equally at home with fast or spin bowling and possesses a variety of strokes on all sides of the wicket. Added to this he is one of the few West Indian batsman who definitely has the Test Match temperament."

That was high praise indeed for someone who had only played in six first-class matches and this, his first outside Jamaica. His selection for the second Test in Trinidad really was a formality and he travelled there on the overnight boat with de Caires. But conditions were quite different: the cricketing fraternity in Trinidad were less exuberant than the Barbadians, and the wicket decidedly less friendly.

The ball bounced higher and turned more on the matting wicket at Queen's Park Oval than he was used to, and Headley struggled to adjust his game, even though he had played on a similar surface in America. However, his spirits were lifted by the arrival of his long-time friend, Tommy Scott, on the island. Headley himself had been somewhat isolated since arriving in Trinidad, as de Caires was housed in separate accommodation, and the Trinidadian players were at home anyway. The two Jamaicans enjoyed practising in the nets together, and were surprised and disappointed when Scott was not selected for the Test side. There was general disapproval in Jamaica too, as Scott had taken time off work and had travelled a long way to make himself available for that game. However, that sort of insensitivity on the part of many of the Caribbean's top cricket administrators was commonplace in those early days.

Perhaps in their defence, it could be said that the selectors preferred to put their faith in indigenous bowlers, as they had recently secured the first victory over the tourists in the colony game. Ironically, however, Trinidad's own batting star, Roach, was going through a bad patch, which was not helped by his captain's decision to move him up and down the batting order. Nelson Betancourt's approach failed in Trinidad's second game against MCC, which the visitors won convincingly, and again in the Test match where Roach made nought opening the first innings and another duck in the second, batting at four. In that match, Headley batted at four in the first innings and had scored just eight runs before he hit his own wicket. Although the Jamaican was the second highest scorer in the second innings with 39, centuries from Patsy Hendren and Les Ames and incisive bowling from Bill Voce earned the tourists a decisive victory.

The England side and some of the West Indians moved on to British Guiana for the third Test, where the hosts had decidedly inferior accommodation to their guests; indeed, Headley and Constantine had to make do with a bed between them. But, even if they had to endure second-class accommodation, the pair were determined to produce a first-class performance. George's spirits were lifted by the sight of the splendid Georgetown wicket and, with Roach having recovered his form, West Indies' prospects looked altogether rosier. The home side batted first and Roach and Errol Hunte put on over 100 for the first wicket, to give Headley an unusually sound base from which to begin his innings. Hunte was dismissed for 53, and Headley was content to play a supporting role to Roach, who was in full flow. The Jamaican finished the first day unbeaten on 60 and returned to his task the next day to add a further 54 runs, after Roach had hoisted the first Test double century for West Indies. These efforts helped the home side to a splendid total of 471, that looked even more impressive once Francis and Constantine had bowled England out for 145.

Surprisingly, the home captain, Maurice Fernandes, declined to enforce the follow-on. Having played so well thus far, the early West Indian batsmen struggled against Wilfred Rhodes and Ewart Astill who kept dropping the ball on a patch just outside the off-stump, that had been worn down by Voce at both ends of the pitch. On a couple of occasions George went down the wicket to take the ball at full pitch and dispatch it to the boundary, and this approach together with freer stroke-play against more orthodox bowling took him to another marvellous century, allowing the West Indians to maintain their grip on the match. Headley delighted in confusing the fielders as he put his left foot to the ball as if to drive through the covers and would then change his stroke at the last minute and cut the ball behind point. Apart from 'Snuffy' Browne, who scored 70, none of the other batsmen supported the master, whose 112 made him the first West Indian to score two separate hundreds in the same Test. But the bowlers, headed by Constantine, capitalised on Headley's good work and, despite a century from Hendren, bowled West Indies to their first Test victory. It was a historic day for West Indian cricket, and Headley had predictably been a key figure.

There was great jubilation in Jamaica when the news reached them that one of their own had become one of cricket's 'immortals', a title accorded to those who score a century in each innings of a Test. Local statisticians started combing through the record books and discovered that Headley was only the fifth man in the history of Test cricket to achieve this feat, after Warren Bardsley of Australia, and the Englishmen, Charles Russell, Herbert Sutcliffe (who had done it twice) and Wally

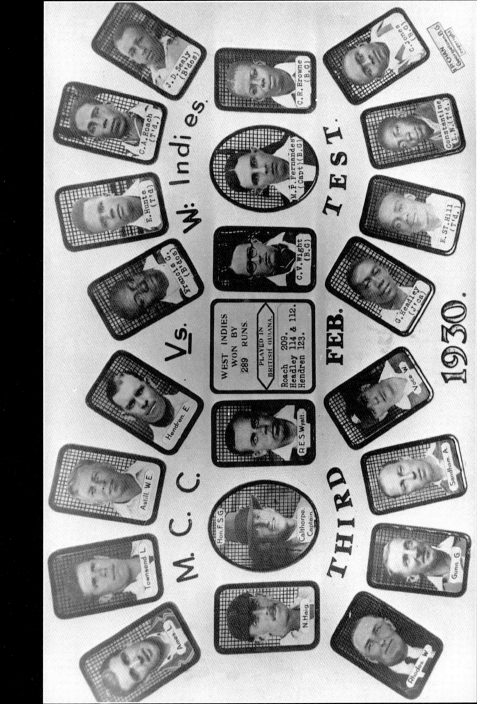

W. Indies. TEST.

M. C. C. Vs. FEB. 1930. THIRD

J. D. Sealy (B'dos)
C. R. Browne (B.G)
C. Jones (B.G)
C. A. Roach (T'd.)
Constantine L. N. (T'd.)
E. Hunte (T'd.)
M. P. Fernandes (Capt.) (B.G)
E. St. Hill (T'd.)
Francis G. (B'dos)
C. V. Wight (B.G)
G. Headley (J'ica)
Hendren E.
WEST INDIES WON BY 289 RUNS.
PLAYED IN BRITISH GUIANA.
Roach 209.
Headley 114 & 112.
Hendren 123.
R. E. S. Wyatt
Voce W
Astill. W. E.
Hon. F. S. G. Calthorpe. Captain.
Sandham A.
Townsend L.
Gunn G.
Ames L.
N. Haig.
Rhodes W

Hammond. However, they had all reached their landmarks in a five-day Test, while Headley had to complete his in four days.

Headley had an enviable technique, keeping his head perfectly still as he played the ball remarkably late, watching its movement until the very last moment. Essentially a back-foot player, he had marvellous balance, and the secret of his batting lay in his impeccable timing as he cut or drove with equal power on both sides of the wicket. Like all great players, he also had a solid defence.

After his extraordinary success in the series to date, there was great anticipation about what the Jamaican maestro would produce for his home crowd in the final Test at Sabina Park. But there were more celebrations to be completed before the team's arrival in Kingston. The ship on which they were travelling from Guiana to Kingston made stops in Colon in Panama, where George had grown up, and Port Limon in Costa Rica. In both places he attended official functions in his honour and received a belt with gold buckle and a purse from the locals, as well as the following address:

❏ *Clifford Roach, who pipped Headley to two impressive batting landmarks.*

Mr George Headley,
Colon, Rep. of Panama
March 12, 1930

Dear Sir,

We the undersigned members of the West Indian colony residing in the Republic of Panama and the Canal Zone have availed ourselves of the opportunity presented by your brief visit to tender to you our warmest congratulations on your brilliant performances in the recent Test matches against the powerful MCC team played in the colonies of Barbados, Trinidad and British Guiana.

We wish at the outset to assure you that this movement to honour you is not an insular affair. On the contrary, representatives of almost every British colony in the Caribbean and Demerara, have worked unitedly in making this reception and presentation possible.

Although domiciled in a foreign land, we are nevertheless keenly interested in everything that tends to the material and social advancement of our homelands. Therefore, we could not permit you to touch this port without manifesting in a tangible form our appreciation of the excellent manner in which you helped to uphold the prestige and traditions of West Indian cricket on the field of Kensington St Clair and Bourda.

When it was learnt that you would be the sole representative of Jamaica in the first Test match at Barbados, the most sanguine amongst us felt that on account of your youth and inexperience in Test matches outside of your island home, and playing as you would under strange surroundings, the best could not be expected from you, but when news was flashed to us that you had made the magnificent score of 176 in the second innings, the jubilation of every West Indian was indescribable.

This function is largely the result of our appreciation of that excellent display. It is true that you did not shine as brilliantly as we had hoped at Trinidad. This no doubt was due to your being unaccustomed to playing on matting. Still, your 39 in the second innings was the second highest score. At Bourda you demonstrated in an unmistakable manner your ability and temperament as a Test match batsman, your 114 first innings and 112 second innings have earned for you undying fame. From a very reliable source we have gathered that you are the fifth batsman in the world that has made over a century in each innings of a Test match. In accomplishing this feat you have carved your name in the niche of fame. To say that we are proud of you is to put it mildly.

It is our sincerest wish that in the series of matches to be played on your native heath you will cover yourself with additional glory. The accompanying souvenir will be presented to you on behalf of the general body of subscribers by Mrs Linda Smart Chubb, a lady highly esteemed in our community life. As you will see, the work has been done in an excellent and artistic manner by Mr R Robinson, a countryman of yours and a well-known jeweller of this city.

It is our hope that this token of our appreciation of your prowess will act as an inspiration to you in your climb to greater renown.

In conclusion we wish to assure you that we shall always follow with interest your career not only as cricketer but also as a man, and that in the years to come your name will be remembered and honoured not only in the land of your nativity, but wherever the grand old English game of cricket is played. Again wishing you continued success and bon voyage.

We are your friends and admirers,

Cyril Lawrence, President.

[The address was signed by over 50 people]

When he finally arrived back in Jamaica, Headley received a rapturous welcome and, after the official ceremonies were over, hurried home to see his aunt. She, like everyone else, was delighted with his success and completed a memorable day by handing him an invitation from the United Fruit Company asking him to be guest of honour at a special function that evening. The event had been arranged by N N McMahon, who had played cricket with George in the St Andrew Police team and with St Catherine and Lucas; Leslie Hylton, then an up-and-coming fast bowler, also played a part in the arrangements. N N 'Crab' Nethersole, who later became a leading political figure in Jamaica, caught the mood when he said: "I have found in a short time that there is nothing like cricket to make a man both earn and appreciate the respect of his fellow men. At this moment Headley is the most distinguished person in Jamaica." At the end of his speech, Nethersole presented George with a sterling silver cup which the staff of the fruit company had bought to commemorate his feat.

The receptions and celebrations seemed endless and must have put considerable pressure on Headley, who was essentially a shy and private man. The Test match at Sabina Park had yet to be played and he gave a hint of his feelings when, accepting the gift from the United Fruit Company, he remarked: "Of course, when one comes off it is said 'Well done, Headley' but when one fails the tendency is to say 'Oh, Headley is no good'."

He performed well in the two colony matches against the tourists played at Melbourne Park, scoring 64, 72 and 52 in his three innings; and also impressed with his close-to-the-wicket fielding, taking five smart catches from the two games.

❏ *Andrew Sandham, who registered the first Test triple century, against West Indies at Sabina Park.*

In keeping with the tradition set in the previous games, the West Indies were captained by an indigenous player. This time the skipper was Karl Nunes who had led the side in England in 1928, and West Indies took the field without the services of Constantine, who was recovering from an operation. As the series was level at that stage, it was decided that the Test match should be played to a finish regardless of time. Freddie Calthorpe won the toss for England and, on a perfect batting wicket, opted to take first strike. By the end of the first day 289 runs had been scored, and West Indies had taken just one wicket. The next day England piled on the agony and eventually totalled 849, thanks to the first Test triple century from Andy Sandham and a single hundred from Les Ames.

The West Indians had lost most of their energy by the time it was their turn to bat and, probably over-awed by England's total, could only muster 286 in reply. Of these Nunes played the best innings, making 66, followed by 44 from Headley's childhood friend, Clarence Passailaigue. Headley himself made just 10. As it was a 'timeless Test', England did not enforce the follow-on but batted on to set the home side a final target of 836.

West Indies had an unsteady start to their second innings, as Roach was dismissed for 22 with just 44 of the runs wiped off. Headley made his way to middle and reassured his skipper that he would not get out so long as Nunes stayed with him. Nunes obliged: by the close of play he had added 30 runs to his score, while the youngster had scored 117; in the end, the pair added 227 for the second wicket, as George stroked his way to a brilliant double hundred, hooking Voce indiscriminately and snatching quick singles off the bowling of Rhodes. He was merciless against anything short and crashed Nigel Haig for three successive boundaries to take West Indies score past 100, and soon overhauled Nunes' score. When the home captain fell eight short of his century the next day, George tightened his game, but the runs continued to flow. When he was finally dismissed for 223, stumped by Ames off the bowling of Bob Wyatt, his score was then the highest ever made by a batsman in the second innings of a Test and the third highest in the history of Test cricket.

When the West Indies had reached 408 for five, rain swept down from the Blue Mountains and continued for two days. With no let-up in sight, the match had to be abandoned - and the series drawn - as the Englishmen had to leave to catch their ship home.

At the end of his first Test series Headley had scored 703 runs at an average of 87.87 from four matches, and became the first batsman to score four Test hundreds before his 21st birthday. Only Sachin Tendulkar has bettered this with seven Test centuries to his credit by the age of 21.

CHAPTER FOUR

AN AUSTRALIAN BAPTISM

I N October 1930 George Headley took his genius outside the Caribbean for the first time, when he left with the West Indies team for their first tour of Australia.

It had been a good preceding season as, thanks to generous public sponsorship, Lucas had acquired their own ground. It was named Nelson Oval after its previous owner; and a memorable year was made complete for Lucas when George, one of their players, was selected to tour Australia. Other Jamaicans in the party were Frank Martin, Ivan Barrow and Tommy Scott. All four boarded the ship to Panama where the touring side were to assemble. When they arrived George took the opportunity of looking up some old pals; in particular he found an old friend called Bailey, who was playing the cornet in a band. The pair reminisced about their sporting youth and some of the cricket enthusiasts in Panama arranged a friendly match between an Isthmian XI and the West Indies team.

For the real contest in Australia, West Indies anticipated that the wickets would be similar to their own, therefore there was an emphasis on fast and medium bowling. Griffith, Francis and Constantine were the nucleus of the attack, with Edwin St Hill the medium-pacer and Scott the slow bowler. Roach, Barrow, Martin and Errol Hunte could all open the innings; George would be at number three and the middle order would be made up of Jackie Grant, the captain, Lionel Birkett, Frank de Caires, Edward Bartlett and Derek Sealy.

The journey from Panama across the Pacific to Australia took a month. It was a calm voyage, so George was not too ill. The team were very disciplined in their fitness programme, engaging in rigorous work-outs and a swim before breakfast then, later in the day, they would practise cricket on deck with improvised nets. It was good experience for them as the wooden deck was faster than a conventional surface, so made them extra sharp.

The West Indians had a brief stop-off at Wellington where they were due to play a New Zealand XI. George, like many of his colleagues, found it difficult to adjust to the change in climate, much preferring the heat of the tropics to the blustery conditions in New Zealand. He also found that in the humid atmosphere of Wellington the ball moved much more than he was used to. The match itself was plagued by intermittent rain, which finally brought it to a premature end. It was a disappointing start for the West Indians, and the New Zealanders were equally put out that their leading batsman, Stewie Dempster, who had made runs against England and Australia, failed to shine. But it was soon time for the West Indians to move on and they took the train to Auckland where they were to board the ship for Sydney.

During the journey the ship ran into a storm in the Tasman Sea which confined George and several of his team mates to their cabins, as their stomachs failed to cope with the vagaries of the sea. But by the time of their arrival in Sydney, the weather had calmed and the cricketers had recovered.

It is important to remember that, given the prevailing attitude over race in those days, it was seen by many as a liberal stance on the part of the Australians to invite the West Indians for a Test series.

Even so, the tourists were reminded of their heritage as soon as they disembarked, when they were given questionnaires to fill in that included a section on race. The Australians were not in the habit of receiving black people in their country and there was mild amusement when one of the black players described himself as 'European'. But once those pedantic issues had been clarified, the welcome from the Australian cricketing fraternity was very warm. Officials from the New South Wales Cricket Association escorted the tour party to their hotel and they were given a formal welcome later that day by the Mayor of Sydney, attended by many distinguished figures, including several cricketers who had retired from the game.

Two such players were Charlie Macartney, who was know as the 'Governor-General' of Australian cricket and one of the few ever to hit a Test century before

❏ *Headley (left) with team mates Derek Sealy and Errol Hunte in Australia, 1931.*

lunch, and Arthur Mailey, once considered the best googly bowler in the world and who had excelled against England. Although they were both retired from the game, they gave the visitors their own special welcome by bowling at them in the nets and offering them advice as they prepared for their first fixture, against the powerful New South Wales team.

New South Wales were Sheffield Shield champions and had a wealth of batting talent at their disposal, including the young Don Bradman, Stan McCabe, who many believed was only slightly behind Bradman in talent, Alan Kippax, a stylist who was considered Australia's finest batsman until the emergence of Bradman and, for good measure, the outstanding Archie Jackson.

The match was keenly fought. West Indies batted first and Roach top-scored with 43, although Headley's 25 was deemed by many to be a masterful innings. He made his runs in less than two overs, albeit Australian overs consisted of eight balls. Indeed, Constantine counted it as one of the finest he had seen Headley play. In the second innings, the Jamaican fell into what was to become his usual role: the backbone of the batting. He top-scored with 82 and only found support from Grant and Constantine, the latter slamming 59. Headley was finally dismissed by a catch from Bradman, and returned the compliment shortly afterwards. However, it was not an entirely one-sided contest and on the final day NSW still needed 89 runs with five wickets in hand. But the issue was never really in doubt after the sixth wicket fell, and McCabe joined Alan Fairfax and knocked off the outstanding runs himself.

The West Indies had far from disgraced themselves and looked forward to the next match against Victoria in Melbourne. George was rather flattered when he arrived to find a morning paper with the headline "How Headley Gets His Runs", complete with diagram indicating his scoring strengths. Only later, as opposing captains started to use the illustration to set fields to Headley, did he realise it was designed to limit his run-scoring.

If they had left the likes of Bradman and McCabe behind in Sydney, the West Indians now had to cope with the might of Bill Ponsford, who had scored over 400 runs in a first-class innings on two occasions. In addition to Ponsford, the West Indians were also intimidated by the slow left-armer, Bert Ironmonger. Apart from George and Learie Constantine, who batted with uncharacteristic caution, the collapse was almost total: Martin was out for three and Roach 10, while de Caires, Grant and Birkett all fell to Ironmonger without scoring. George responded as only he could by increasing his scoring rate. Constantine propped up the other end for some considerable time with 34, as Headley scored at three times the Trinidadian's rate. In the end, he hit 131 runs out of a total of 212, in an innings that was hailed as one of the finest ever seen on the historic Melbourne ground, where giants of the past, including Victor Trumper, had been seen in full flow.

In reply Victoria scored 594, aided by 187 from Ponsford, although his innings was dour compared to the likes of Headley or Bradman. In the second innings George top-scored with 34 before he was adjudged LBW to Ironmonger, who took eight for 31, as the tourists crumbled to 128 all out. The Trinidad *Sporting Chronicle*, responding to the news of the innings defeat, wrote "the performance of George Headley was the losers' saving grace...the chief glory of his cricket is his power of punishing slow bowling...he follows the old rule of getting to the pitch of the ball and uses straight drives to the sightscreen...small, beautifully set, with an ease and poise that denotes one essential foundation of good batsmanship - perfect co-ordination of the limbs."

The *Sporting Globe* of Melbourne could hardly contain its enthusiasm. Under the heading "George Headley One Of the Outstanding Batsmen of the World" and extravagant sub-heading "Of Bradman's Type But With More Polish. An Innings To Be More Remembered", it reported: "Everyone who saw the West Indians batting against Victoria on Friday agreed that in George Headley, aged 21 years, they had one of the outstanding batsmen of the day.

"We have seen many wonderful English and Australian batsmen in action on the Melbourne ground, but we have seen very few finer displays of batting than this Jamaican boy gave us on Friday. There was the unmistakable mark of the class batsman in every stroke and every movement.

"There was no stroke in the batsman's range that he did not accomplish with grace and ease. He made a quiet beginning, but it was not long before he was putting force into his strokes, and a forceful innings it continued to be - force with polish in the making of every stroke, from the late and square cut to the full-blooded drive and the dainty leg-glance. Throughout it all he was the complete master of the bowling, and never looked like being in trouble, and even when forced on to a defensive stroke he executed it in a way that indicated a lack of difficulty or danger. Perfect timing, beautiful wrist work, and footwork that was a model, made the ball fly from the bat, sometimes in an astonishing way.

"It was an innings that will be remembered for many years by those who saw it. Reports of his batting in the Tests against the Englishmen in the West Indies recently indicated that he was rather a slow scorer, therefore his delightfully free display in this innings came as something of a surprise. Not for nothing has he been called the Bradman of the West Indies. He is a batsman of Bradman's type, but with more polish. It seems certain that he is going to give our bowlers a tremendous lot of trouble this season. He already is among the great batsmen of the world and it is conceivable that he will rise to the very greatest heights in the near future."

Despite Headley's remarkable performances, by this time, the West Indian team as a whole were feeling somewhat brow-beaten, but made their way to Adelaide where they were to play South Australia. Although the South Australians did not have such a strong batting complement, they did enjoy the services of Clarrie Grimmett, who had succeeded Mailey as Australia's best slow bowler. He, too, was helped by the newspaper diagram showing George's scoring strengths which had been reproduced in the local paper on the first morning of the game. In that match, for the first time in his career, Headley began to struggle. He found that it was difficult to get the ball away because the bowlers were attacking his leg-stump to a well-placed leg-side field. Grimmett was particularly hard to hit, as loose balls from him were a rarity. George was tied down in a way he had not known before and had managed only 27 when he was run out, and just 16 in the second innings. West Indies' totals of 171 and 162 reflected his poor showing and the South Australians won by 10 wickets.

Although their defeat was comprehensive, the West Indians were already showing some of the famous Australian competitiveness. This was demonstrated by Herman Griffith when, with the hosts requiring just four runs for victory in the second innings, he bowled a maiden over.

Even so, they must have felt nervous with the first Test at Adelaide looming. Australia, under the captaincy of Bill Woodfull, were able to call on a splendid array of talent: in the batting department there was Bradman, Ponsford, Kippax, McCabe, Jackson and Fairfax; in the bowling, there were the slow men, Grimmett and Alec Hurwood, with Tim Wall the sole fast bowler, and Bert Oldfield the wicket-keeper.

Against this formidable line-up, West Indies could pit Grant, Headley, Roach, Bartlett, Birkett and Martin as the batsmen; their trio of fast bowlers Constantine, Francis and Griffith, who would be supported by slow bowlers, Scott and Martin, while Barrow kept wicket.

The match began in sweltering heat and the ground was packed with eager spectators; West Indies won the toss and elected to bat. They scored 296 largely due to the efforts of Roach, Grant and Bartlett. George felt in fine form but fell first ball to Grimmett, who took seven for 87 in the innings. Australia replied with 376, a total that could have been substantially reduced if the good bowling had been backed by comparable fielding. The visitors' cause was not helped when Kippax was dropped on nine and went on to 146. In the second innings the tourists scored 249, aided by another captain's innings from Grant.

Headley was again pinned down by Grimmett, who was bowling to a packed leg-side field, and obliged to play out several maiden overs to shield Birkett from the guiles of Grimmett, who was scoring well off Wall. But Headley's

❏ *Clarrie Grimmett, whose style of bowling foiled Headley in the early part of the Australian tour.*

patience finally ran out and he was stumped off the spinner going after a well-flighted ball, with his score on 11. Tommy Scott consoled him in the dressing-room, explaining that Grimmett was tired after bowling so many maidens: "He kidded you and you fell for it. Good batsman as you are, the bowler must get you out rather than you get yourself out." It was at this point that George remembered the advice of Constantine before he played his first Test match, "play within your limitations". In the end, Australia needed only 172 to win and scored them without incident, Ponsford making 92 and Jackson 70. Even though they were out-played, the West Indians were disappointed that the wicket, once reputed to be one of the best batting strips in Australia, had played so slowly.

From Adelaide, the tourists took the train to Melbourne and the ship to Tasmania. It was very cold on the southern island and George saw snow for the first time. Despite the temperature, West Indies lifted their game and their spirits when they won their first game of the tour at Launceston, thanks largely to a century from Constantine. There was a second game at Hobart, but it was spoiled by the weather. Even so their morale was high as they boarded the ship for the return journey to Sydney to await the second Test, beginning on New Year's Day.

The match was played on an easy-paced wicket, but thoughtful bowling from Griffith put West Indies briefly on top. However, 183 from Ponsford helped Australia to 369, which proved way beyond the tourists who were over-awed by the bowling of Grimmett, Hurwood and Fairfax. George failed to lift himself out of his low-scoring impasse, making just 14 and two, and West Indies' paltry totals of 107 and 90 ensured they collapsed to an innings defeat.

The story goes that their defeat came as a particular disappointment to an

❏ *'The Don', who was affectionately known as the 'White Headley' in Jamaica.*

Englishman called Walter Abbott. The director of a shoe company and an ardent West Indies supporter, he had accompanied them on their first tour of Australia. He was a great fan of George's and offered him £20 for every Test century he made. At the beginning of the second Test he put five gold pieces in George's pocket for luck. But when his good luck charm failed to work he returned to England and never made contact with the West Indies team again!

By this stage of the tour there was a feeling that, perhaps, the contest was too one-sided and the number of Tests should be cut. The team themselves had very little time to think in those terms as most of their time was taken up with practice sessions, matches and the huge distances that had to be covered between the different venues.

Their next stop was Brisbane for a match against Queensland, which was a long haul up from Sydney. But the tourists enjoyed the change in climate and the tropical fruits during the upward journey. A feature of the match against Queensland was the outstanding bowling of an Aborigine named Gilbert. He was able to generate a lot of pace from an extremely short run and had an enviable attitude to the game, running up to Constantine and shaking his hand when he hit a six off his bowling, explaining that that was the first time anyone had hit him for six. Constantine again made match-winning contributions with 75 and 97 although, once more, George was not in the runs. The Jamaican was struggling, having put on weight over Christmas, and realised he must work to revive his game before the third Test. Fortunately for the West Indies, he was back to his best for that match.

Even so, it was Bradman's turn to excel first. Australia won the toss and elected to bat and compiled a score of 558 due in the main to a majestic double hundred from The Don. Headley had in fact missed him on four - probably the most costly dropped catch of his career - and this innings together with a century from Ponsford put Australia in a commanding position. By the end of the first day they had scored well over 300 runs for the loss of just three wickets and it needed incisive bowling from the West Indians on the second day to stem the flow of runs.

West Indies went in to bat and had a mere five on the board before Roach was dismissed. The Australians were anticipating another substantial victory by maintaining their leg-side bowling tactics, but this time they came unstuck. Headley had been working on his game and had a different approach even though the batsmen at the other end, including Grant and Constantine, were succumbing to the Australian attack. George proved himself to be in a different class. Slowly he gained in confidence and was soon finding the boundary with increasing regularity. His fluency eventually persuaded Grimmett to alter his strategy: he abandoned his leg-trap and placed two slips 15 feet from George and attacked his off-stump. But George would not be tempted and declined anything outside the off-stump. He played a brilliant, chanceless innings and Barrow stayed long enough at the wicket for George to complete his hundred. But he only just managed it: he played a late cut off Grimmett for two runs, before Francis and then Griffith were bowled. He finished unbeaten on 102 out of a total of 193, and thereby became the first West Indian to score a Test hundred against Australia.

The secret of his success lay in his new two-eyed stance, that he had adopted to combat the leg-side field, and which allowed him more opportunity to place the ball between the fielders. So sparkling was his play that Bradman and McCabe were two of the first visitors to come to the dressing-room to congratulate him on his performance. Incidentally, the Jamaican bowler, Arthur Bonitto, believed he got many extra wickets after this because young batsmen imitated the first part of George's stance but failed to get into his orthodox position when making contact with the ball.

That night George got very little sleep, as it seemed abnormally hot even by Queensland standards. The players soon found out why the next day: there had been a volcanic eruption in New Zealand and the effects had reached Brisbane. Meanwhile, in the match itself, West Indies were obliged to follow-on, and George was soon batting again. He had made 28 when McCabe remarked to him at the end of the over that it looked like he would get another century. George was amused and then tried to glance a ball from Ironmonger that pitched just outside the leg-stump, but he got a thin edge to the wicket-keeper. His lapse in concentration contributed to West Indies losing the match, but George learnt from the incident and never took that chance again.

C L R James illustrates Headley's thought-processes graphically in an imaginary scenario in *Beyond a Boundary*: "George is batting against an Australian slow bowler, probably Grimmett. To the length ball he gets back and forces Grimmett away between mid-wicket and mid-on or between mid-wicket and square-leg. He is so quick on his feet and so quick with his bat that Grimmett simply cannot stop ones and twos in between the fieldsmen. Every time Grimmett flights the ball, out of the crease and the full drive. Grimmett, that great master of length, can't even keep George quiet. He has a man at fine leg. He shifts him round to square and moves square to block up the hole. Next ball is just outside the leg-stump. George, gleeful at the thought that fine-leg is no longer there, dances in front of the wicket 'to pick up a cheap four'. He glances neatly, only to see Oldfield, the wicket-keeper, way over on the leg-side taking the catch. The two seasoned Australians have trapped him. That sort of thing has happened often enough. Now note George's reaction:

'I cut it out.'

'What do you mean, you cut it out?'

'I just made up my mind never to be caught that way again.'

'So you do not glance?'

'Sure I glance, but I take care to find out first if any of these traps are being laid.'

'Always?'

'Always.'

And I can see he means it."

After the third Test, the tourists were due to play a second match against Victoria where George had done so well before. The Victorians were under-strength for that match which meant the West Indians could be more relaxed in their approach and play with more bravado. Roach and Headley, in particular, excelled, Roach collecting a century and George making 77. Grant and de Caries also made runs, to help West Indies to a total of 495. Victoria replied with 325 and West Indies rattled up 238 for five, with Headley scoring 113. In the end, the visitors just failed to force a victory as the game ended with Victoria nine wickets down and still requiring 128 runs.

After Melbourne it was back to South Australia, where the weather was now pleasantly warm. By this time the West Indians generally were coping more successfully with the Australian slow bowlers. Although Headley was once again dismissed by Grimmett, he could not induce a mistake until George had made 75, while a century from Grant, 63 from Constantine and 34 from Bartlett helped West Indies to 383. South Australia could only manage 278 in reply. West Indies then made 208, with George scoring 39, but South Australia scraped home in a thrilling one-wicket victory. Had Constantine not injured himself and been unable to bowl the result might have been different.

The fourth Test at Melbourne was a disaster for the tourists. They lost by an innings, falling mostly to Ironmonger, and it was small consolation to George that he had scored exactly one third of his side's runs in the first innings by making 33. His failure in the second innings condemned West Indies to a comprehensive defeat.

❑ *Jackie Grant, whose imaginative captaincy at Sydney secured West Indies' first Test victory in Australia.*

By this time it had transpired that the tour was also losing money, so economy measures were introduced. One of these was that the tourists had to go to practice sessions by tram-cars rather than taxis, but this was no real hardship and gave them an opportunity to meet the locals.

By that stage of the tour George had become friendly with several members of the Australian side and got on particularly well with Stan McCabe who, like himself, was one of the younger members of the team. Whenever he was in Sydney the pair would often visit the home of Chappie Dwyer, who had first noticed McCabe's potential and who also served on the Australian Board of Control. When the West Indians returned to Sydney for the final Test, George met Chappie and mentioned that they had been anticipating wickets of a similar pace to those in the Caribbean. Apart from when they played their opening match on a fast wicket against New South Wales, George felt the wickets had been doctored and implored Chappie to produce some faster wickets so the Australian public could see better cricket. His pleas were supported by Constantine and Scott who joined the discussion.

Dwyer relayed the conversation to the authorities in Sydney and it seems some effort was made to prepare faster wickets. Buoyed by the pace of the pitch, the West Indies capitalised on the improved conditions and helped themselves to 339 in the penultimate match of the tour against New South Wales. Roach played freely, George top-scored with 70 and Sealy also came into his own. The pace of Constantine, ably supported by Griffith, then skittled the opposition out for 190. In the second innings, Sealy and Constantine both made nineties and Scott scored an unbeaten 67. These performances helped West Indies to 403 for nine and a seemingly invincible position. However, NSW batted with more resolve second time round: Bradman scored a determined 73, Kippax 141 and McCabe 100. In the end, persistent bowling from Francis, who collected four wickets for 76, secured victory for West Indies by 86 runs.

The West Indies went into the final Test at Sydney in euphoric mood. Things went well for them from the start: they won the toss and elected to bat. Despite tight bowling from the Australians, supported by keen fielding, the first day was a good one for the West Indies and Jamaica in particular. Headley and Frank Martin both scored centuries and by this stage Headley was playing Grimmett with such fluency that the latter was moved to remark that George was the best on-side batsman he had ever bowled to, and he bowled against both Jack Hobbs and Bradman himself. During his innings George became only the 12th touring batsman to score 1,000 runs in an Australian season, and this after his miserable start.

Late on the first day rain began to fall, prompting Jackie Grant to declare on 350 for six early on the second morning as West Indies lost four quick wickets (beginning with his own after he had made 62), with Martin unbeaten on 123; George had fallen LBW to McCabe for 105. Despite the nature of the wicket, Australia fought bravely: Bradman made a gallant 43, while 54 from Alan Fairfax helped the home side to 224. In their second innings the tourists reached 124 for five before rain intervened again. Given that Australia had batted so well in poor conditions, Grant knew that a second declaration was risky, but he had great faith in his bowlers and decided to take the chance. They responded magnificently, Griffith in particular bowled well and finished with four for 50 including the prized wicket of Bradman, who made the first duck of his Test career. Constantine also played a significant part in making sure the home side did not reach their target by taking three catches. A stubborn partnership between McCabe and Fairfax threatened to prevent a historic victory for West Indies, but once Martin had accounted for McCabe there was little more resistance.

Almost as soon as victory had been posted, another storm blew up and the ground was quickly submerged in water. But the West Indies were safe and had created history by become the first side ever to win a Test after making two declarations.

So they ended the tour on a high note, and learned much of the Australian character that would stand them in good stead in future series. They were given an enthusiastic farewell as they boarded their ship for New Zealand, although Grant left his team at that stage bound for Rhodesia, where he was to take up missionary work. The West Indians changed ship at Wellington and crossed the Pacific Ocean in the SS Mataroa. When they reached Cristobal in Panama two delegates from the West Indian community in Panama boarded and accompanied them through the canal to Colon. There a large delegation greeted them at the pier and the cricketers were escorted by over 1,000 West Indian-Panamanians through the streets thronged with people. They were given a champagne reception by the Atlantic Cricket Council at the Ideal Auditorium.

It was at Colon that the players went their separate ways, those from the Eastern

❏ A dapper George Headley in relaxed mood in Sydney, 1931.

Caribbean going one way and the Jamaicans another. As the Jamaicans were in Colon for a few days a match was hurriedly organised by the locals, so they could compete against the men they had read so much about. In that match, played at Mount Hope Ball Park, George revealed his prowess as a bowler, capturing two wickets. Thereafter Headley, Ivan Barrow, Frank Martin and Tommy Scott began the third and final leg of their journey home. As ever, they received an enthusiastic welcome when they arrived in Port Royal as cricket officials, the Press, friends and relations greeted them; and went on to a reception attended by the Governor of Jamaica, the President of the Cricket Board and other leading figures.

Obviously delighted to be home, they made no excuse for their difficulties other than remarking that the wickets were slower than expected. They had lavish praise for their opponents - Bradman and McCabe in particular - and George remarked that cricket in Australia was "entirely different to what I have played in the past, and I think I was somewhat lucky in being able to adapt myself to a means of getting my runs". He elaborated on the competitive Australian nature: "You get no half-volleys and if you have one good scoring shot off which you generally get runs you are blocked all the while, or at least they concentrate on blocking you as far as that channel is concerned."

The Australians, Bradman in particular, had been equally complimentary about the visitors. Bradman told the Press that he was "sure that not only cricket of the West Indian team but also that of Australia has been improved through this visit." He regarded Constantine as one of the world's leading all-rounders and had words of praise for Francis and Griffith. He felt George had lived up to his reputation and admired the way in which he overcame his difficulties against Clarrie Grimmett early on in the tour. At the time he observed the great power in his shots that, given his small physique, must have derived from perfect timing. His only criticism of George was his running between the wickets which Bradman thought all the West Indians needed to pay attention to.

But of all the praise lavished on Headley and of all the official functions he attended the one that left him with fondest memories was when he was invited back to Calabar Elementary School by the strait-laced Principal, H A Stephenson. It was a nostalgic occasion for George, attended by many of his old school pals and his last teacher, Miss Banton. An unusually relaxed Mr Stephenson addressed the expectant assembly of children: "Old students of Calabar, teachers, boys and girls. Not so long ago George Headley was sitting on one of those benches in sixth class, being taught by Miss Banton. He grew up in this school just as you are doing, and I remember he used to love to play chevy-chase during the recess. We noted his talent at cricket when he represented this school against All Saints, St Michael's and others. But little did we think that he would be representing Jamaica as he did against Lord Tennyson's team. He performed well then, and you don't need me to describe how well he batted in the Test matches against England. I personally wondered how he would acquit himself when he toured Australia. Well, he made over 1,000 runs there and we have invited him here today to congratulate him. Now we have put together all the quatties, pennies and farthings you contributed and bought him a token of our appreciation. I will now ask Miss Banton to present it to him." Miss Banton then presented her most famous pupil with a pair of cuff links.

CHAPTER FIVE

1932: A WORLD RECORD YEAR

G EORGE had grown up in Australia. He played against men who made the opposition work, and often struggle, for every wicket and run. But he had come through the experience with flying colours and had won the respect and admiration of many of the finest players of his day.

The thrill of succeeding at the highest level and the morale-boosting effect it had on his country inspired him to lift his game to even greater heights. Even if he hadn't decided to set new targets for himself, the crowds now expected him to perform on every occasion he went into bat. Their impatience was heightened by the fact that they hadn't seen him play at first-class level in Jamaica for two years. Two of his last major appearances at home had brought him double centuries: against Lord Tennyson's team at Melbourne Park in 1928 and against England in the Test at Sabina Park in 1930; now they wanted more.

The fortunes of Lucas CC on his return from Australia were typified by their first match. A huge crowd assembled at the Kensington Club to watch George play his first innings since returning from Australia. He did not disappoint them, scoring 31 not out. The following week, however, it was a different story: he strolled to the wicket only to be dismissed first ball. In the end Lucas made 167, failing by one run to tie the Kensington score. In the play-off that followed Lucas defeated Railway, but lost to Kensington.

Once the Senior Cup season was completed, George travelled to the United States to play some more exhibition matches,

❏ *The garish Percy Chapman, who hoped to do better against Headley's golden blade than previous English teams.*

❏ *The 1932 Jamaican team... Standing (l-r): Ivan Barrow, Ernest Rae, Clarence Passailaigue, Karl Nunes, Vin Valentine, Leslie Hylton. Sitting (l-r): Tommy Scott, W G Beckford, George Headley, Oscar da Costa, Ken Weekes.*

along with his Lucas team mates Stanley Mulvaney and Archie Whittingham and W G Beckford of St Catherine and H B Young of Kensington. He enjoyed the cricket away from the pressures of competition, and was able to visit his family again.

On his return home George was delighted to hear that Lord Tennyson was making his fourth trip to Jamaica. In preparation for the visit George ran and swam regularly in addition to having regular nets, and enjoyed the services of a masseur, who would bike down to the beach to limber him up after his swim.

George was given an added lift at the start of that season, with the news that he was to captain Lucas in the Senior Cup matches. A good showing in the Jamaica trial matches completed his build-up for the arrival of Tennyson's team. The Lord arrived at Port Royal with his side that included the England captain, Percy Chapman, and immediately lived up to his gregarious reputation. Adorned in a gaudy dressing-gown, he told the Jamaican Press that he planned to give their team "a real licking" as he had brought a very strong side with him.

His Lordship, donning a felt hat, had a promising start to the tour, making 40 against a Jamaica Next XI captained by 'Crab' Nethersole. A huge crowd assembled at Melbourne Park to watch the first match between Tennyson's men and the full Jamaica side. There was a buzz of expectancy in the air as the captains, Tennyson and Nunes, went out to toss up. Jamaica won and Beckford and Ivan Barrow opened the batting for the home side. The innings had been going for a mere six minutes, with one run on the board, before Beckford was run out. The Jamaica maestro had never said a truer word than when he remarked, "I would be putting on my pads and sometimes before I was finished I would hear that the first wicket had gone".

He underlined the discrepancy between himself and the rest of the team and, indeed, everyone else on the field, by getting off the mark with a boundary and proceeded to attack the bowling without mercy. He was on 30 before Barrow reached 10, and then shared in a partnership of 32 with Nunes before lunch, of which the captain's contribution was one run. Indeed the loss of Barrow and Nunes in quick succession before the interval only seemed to strengthen his resolve to take the attack to the English. Partnered by Oscar da Costa, he hit a four past mid-on to take Jamaica's total to 100 and not long after reached his own century in exactly the same fashion, with his 15th four. 'The Young Master', a name he had been given by the Press, was certainly living up to his reputation.

Headley gave a hard caught and bowled chance to Ewart Astill when he was on 110 but, far from accepting the catch, Astill was knocked over by the force of the shot and suffered further when, seemingly oblivious to George's success against Clarrie Grimmett in Australia, he bowled at his leg-stump to a packed on-side field. That provided George with further rich-pickings. He had reached 130 when he lost da Costa, who had played well for 26.

The next man in was Clarence Passailaigue, his long-standing friend, nicknamed 'the Broom' for his knack of sweeping a ball on the off-stump to the leg-side boundary. He had played in the last Test in the Caribbean, at Kingston in 1930. 'Pass' started quietly but, encouraged by the success of George, soon adopted a more attacking pose. Inspired by having a partner who seemed prepared to adopt his style, Headley lifted his game into another gear and cut and drove his way to within reach of a second century as, for a while, the pair scored at a rate of almost two runs a minute. Before he reached the landmark he appeared to tire, but once he had passed 190 the adrenalin started to flow again as he surged towards 200. There seemed to be no stopping him: he went on and on, passed his previous best score of 211 against Lord Tennyson's side, made at Melbourne Park in 1928, passed the 223 he had made in the Test at Sabina Park, then passed Nunes' record Senior Cup score of 227 and, all the while, Passailaigue obliged by keeping the score ticking over at his end. They finished the day with George on 236 not out and Clarence unbeaten on 157; the crowd ran on to the field and practically carried their heroes into the pavilion.

They continued in the same vein the next day and might have batted on for a week if Nunes hadn't declared the innings closed on 702 for five with Headley on 344 not out (40 more than the highest first-class score previously made by a West Indian, when Tim Tarilton had made a triple century for Barbados against Trinidad in 1919-20, and 19 more than the highest score previously made in the West Indies, when Sandham scored his triple Test hundred) and Passailaigue on 261 not out. Their partnership of 487 remains the world record for the sixth wicket: George hit 39 fours in his innings and batted for 407 minutes, while the side as a whole had produced its total in 413 minutes; Passailaigue had crashed one six and 37 fours in his innings and only taken 248 minutes for his runs. Coincidentally the score of the two Jamaicans totalled the same as Tennyson's team in their innings' defeat, 354 and 251.

It was a day of great celebration in Jamaica and the two local heroes posed for photographs in front of the Jamaica mascot, an effigy of a crocodile resting on a table, covered by the national flag. The English fielders, having witnessed a remarkable display of world class batting, were generous in their praise. Morris Nichols put it in perspective: "You bowl your best to Headley and it isn't enough, so you try and bowl better than your best, and he hits you for four!" The *Daily Gleaner* wrote: "Of the bowling itself it is hard to form an opinion, for a genius of the game such as Headley is a tremendous handicap to any bowling side." In the end Jamaica won by an innings and 97 runs although, to his credit, Tennyson still said he was hoping to even things up in the next match.

To celebrate the world record achieved in that game, G B Beckford wrote the poem reproduced on the facing page:

The English XI seemed determined to make it more of a contest in the second match at Sabina Park, and began promisingly by scoring 402. Then their bowlers were quickly on top, in particular the googly bowler Greville Stevens, and the home side were dismissed for 228. Of those, George top-scored with 84, with the only real support coming from 'Crab' Nethersole who made 49. The hosts lifted themselves in the second innings, as Tommy Scott's six for 91 helped to skittle the visitors out for 188. Jamaica began her second innings with the game finely balanced. Nunes and Clausie Boy started well, before centuries from the captain and Headley gave Jamaica a firm grip on the match. However, Nunes' dismissal for 125 pre-empted a minor collapse, as two more wickets fell immediately after. But da Costa arrived at the wicket to stop the rot and stayed with Headley until his side were within two runs of victory.

Jamaica's new boy, D P Beckford, walked to the wicket and managed to squeeze one run from the bowling of Stevens. By then, Headley had had enough of this

HEADLEY G AND CLARENCE P
AT MELBOURNE PARK 1932

I see a glorious spreading field with beautiful trees around
while here and there beneath the shade keen cricketers abound
I hear a mighty thund'rous cheer...loud cries of 'Headley G'
and the figures on the Board declare a 'treble century'.
I see a dapper pleasant guy, while the crowd's expectant...tense
with clever play, drive the ball away careering to the fence;
And now, it is GEARY bowling down; mayhap the bails will fall,
but HEADLEY G steps out quite free and sends it o'er the wall.

Now cries of 'STEVENS'! rend the air, 'cleverest bowler of the side'
but off his first - it could be worse - a shout goes up: 'one wide'!
And then he tries a tricky one, while fielders spread the more,
but HEADLEY G exclaims 'Not me'! and strikes the ball for four.
See another broader guy, with rare spontaneity
request more room to wield his broom for a double century,
And peering o'er Mass Charlie's gate, think it best to bring
the presence of a cricket ball direct to him on wing.

But how the scorers weary work, the bowlers hope and change
the fieldsmen blown upon the hunt for balls without their range;
I see the ball rise o'er the trees...on road...o'er fence...in stand
I see it skimming 'bove the ground on peering heads to land.

I hear the shout...the constant of the excited throng,
as HEADLEY G and CLARENCE P make bowler bowl all wrong;
And in my dreams I see them still, play at will and free -
CLARENCE P, the Hurricane Broom and competent HEADLEY G.

tension and drove Stevens' next ball to long-on for a single, before making a quick dash for the pavilion, as the police were obliged to keep over-enthusiastic well-wishers at bay. George had scored 155 not out and at that stage of the series was averaging 583!

Lord Tennyson must have thought his chances of success greatly improved when Jamaica fielded a side without Nunes or Scott for the final game. In optimistic mood the tourists scored 333 in their first innings and would have done even better but for the accuracy of Leslie Hylton, who took four English wickets for 55.

George maintained his brilliant form when Jamaica batted. The visitors had abandoned their idea of attacking his leg-stump and he scored freely on both sides of the wicket. He completed a predictable century, punctuated by some sweetly-timed boundaries, and shared in a glorious partnership of 248 with Barrow, who top-scored with 169 in Jamaica's total of 561. In the end, Jamaica romped home: requiring 133 to win, they reached their target with four wickets to spare and George still in the pavilion.

In those days there was no Man of the Series award but, if there had have been, there was no doubt who would have taken the prize: George's aggregate for the series was 723 runs (more than Tennyson's team totalled in both innings of any one match) for an average of 361.50 (more than Tennyson's team scored in five of their six innings), made over a period of just 23 days, and only Bradman of other batsmen had ever made over 700 runs in four consecutive innings. Lord Tennyson summed up the feeling of many when, speaking of George's batting in that series, he said: "I cannot recollect such perfection of timing nor a variety of shots and the delight of it all was that he himself was, I am sure, unconscious that he was doing anything out of the ordinary."

Having failed to stop him as a batsman, the likeable Lord tried to win him over with his poetry. Some time later, after George had agreed to play for Haslingden in the Lancashire League, Tennyson tried to entice him to his old club, Hampshire, with the following (right):

> Twinkle, twinkle, ebon head,
> With your average so high.
> How we wondered how to get you
> In the Test just now gone by.
>
> When next year you come to England,
> Don't give Haslingden a glance;
> Let me beg, beseech, implore you -
> Stay and twink a bit for Hants.

At last Jamaica had a star, a black star, for the indigenous population to look up to. If their own lives were often hard and unrewarding at least they could take heart from the fact that 'one of their own' had made it. Headley was their first sporting hero, which made him all the more special; the boxing superstars and athletic champions had yet to emerge. As the editor of the *Daily Gleaner*, H G Delisser, put it: "Even the non-cricketer cannot fail to be struck by the devotion of Jamaica to cricket - to hear urchins along the street, labourers, persons of every class...discussing the game now being played with knowledge, interest and fervour is a continued revelation of the way in which cricket has taken upon the people of Jamaica."

The business community was not slow to get in on the act either. Realising they had a very marketable product, William Sykes Limited, who had made the bat Headley used in his record-breaking innings, asked him to autograph some of their bats; while the Nestlé Milk Company were equally keen to earn publicity by being associated with a great sportsman and presented him with a three-handled solid silver cup with the inscription: "To George Headley, in recognition of His Splendid Batting and his service to Jamaica Cricket".

More importantly, three prominent businessmen, Messrs Alexander, Morais and Seymour-Seymour formed a committee to try to raise funds to keep George in Jamaica as a professional cricketer, so that he would not have to accept offers to play league cricket in England. But, after 1933, these approaches came thick and fast and were better than anything offered in Jamaica.

Headley rounded off a wonderful season by leading Lucas to success in the Senior Cup, the first time they had won the trophy since 1915. There had been so many teams in the competition that they had been divided into two zones and, after collecting most points in their zone thanks to two fine hundreds from George against Kingston CC, Lucas then beat Melbourne CC, captained by Ivan Barrow, to secure the trophy, with George scoring 107. By the end of that season, Headley had scored 2,317 runs from 40 innings at an average of 64.08.

❏ *The Jamaican master making a characteristically flamboyant shot.*

❏ *Pictured with admiring onlookers at Liverpool during the 1933 tour.*

CHAPTER SIX
WEST INDIES EXPECT

N 1933 West Indies held trials for the first time to help select the team for the coming tour to England. They took place on the matting wickets at Port-of-Spain in the belief that they were the most similar to English wickets. On that occasion, Headley's selection really was a foregone conclusion, although he was concerned that Derek Sealy was not included in the tour party.

But he had no say in selection matters and boarded the ship for the Eastern Caribbean. There were several stops en route to Barbados, and when he arrived on the island he decided to get out for a look round. However, rummaging through his baggage he realised he had forgotten his passport. The Jamaican officials did not ask for it when he left home, so he was obliged to cable his aunt and ask her to send it on to England. Fortunately when he arrived at Southampton, the English custom officials were able to hand it to him. It was the last service his aunt was able to do for him, as she died while he was on tour.

When they arrived in England, the climate was very different. The tropical warmth and brilliant sunshine of the West Indies became a distant memory, as they got used to the greyer atmosphere of England. They travelled from Southampton to London and were met by officials from the MCC and, having settled in their hotels and bought suitable clothing, went to Lord's for their first practice session. George was impressed by the splendour of the ground and spent some time in the historic Long Room: it all seemed a long way from Crabhole Park!

With the likes of Herbert Sutcliffe, Wally Hammond, Maurice Leyland, Les Ames and Douglas Jardine on hand for England there was no shortage of class batsmen vying with George for attention. There was great anticipation about how he would fare in the variable climatic conditions and on the softer English wickets, although the reputable *Manchester Guardian* thought he would measure up, pointing out that only Bradman had done better than 'the Big Noise' as E W Swanton referred to him, (interestingly R C Robertson-Glasgow believed Headley's art had no noise!)

The master played well from the beginning, scoring 83 against a Club Cricket Conference XI and 52 out of a West Indies total of 129 on a wet wicket against Northamptonshire, hooking anything short to the boundary.

On his first appearance at Lord's, he scored 129 against MCC, but was injured in the second innings when he was hit in the chest by a ball from Bill Bowes that forced him to miss the next three games. Even so, he had impressed sufficiently in the first innings to prompt the following comment: "He is just Headley, a little man, neat and quick on his feet, sturdily orthodox on the whole, who plays even his defensive strokes hard. On Saturday he seldom lifted the ball an inch, but his drives cracked to the boundary with a giant's force. The power of his hitting was astonishing for so small a man and he does not put a big amount of swing into his strokes. The secret of his force is perfect timing."

Already Headley had adjusted to the pace of the wicket and the effect that humidity had on the bowling; on his return after injury he batted with great assurance for 129 against Glamorgan and 224 not out against Somerset in successive innings. A second double hundred against Derbyshire saw him to 1,000 first-class runs on 15 June. He was invariably at his best on wet wickets and top-scored for his side against Yorkshire, Nottinghamshire, Lancashire and Leicestershire in such conditions. Constantine later recalled the tussle during the Yorkshire match between West Indies' Headley, George, and Yorkshire's Hedley, Verity: "Headley came out. He meant business, and hooked the first ball to square leg. It would certainly have been a boundary, but Dipper the umpire was not quick enough, and both of them were justly incensed...How Verity enjoyed that wet wicket! He could do what he liked with the ball, spin it quickly away, make it lift or turn - and we could do nothing with him. For a long time there was a personal duel between Verity and Headley. It was a cricket education to watch them. Verity would bowl an innocent-looking thing that had all the wiles of the devil in it. Headley would play back quietly. The next ball he would jump right out and send to the extra cover boundary. Then the attack would alter. Verity got him at last...he always got you at last on a wicket like that. But Headley had collected 25 in one of the most *skilful* innings I have ever seen played."

C L R James also recalled that match: "One day in 1933 West Indies were playing Yorkshire at Harrogate, the wicket was wet and Verity placed men close in, silly mid-off and silly point I think. The West Indian players talked about the bowlers who placed men close in for this batsman and the other batsman. George joined in the reminiscences. Someone said, 'George, if Verity put a man there for you...'

"A yell as of sudden, intense, unbearable pain burst from George, so as to startle everyone for yards around.

"'Me!' he said. 'Put a man there for me!'

"They could talk about it for other players, Test players, but that anyone should even think that such fieldsmen could be placed for him - that was too much for George. The idea hurt him physically."

George enjoyed great success in the Test series. Even though the West Indies lost the first match at Lord's by an innings, Headley's second innings 50 was the highest score by a visiting batsman in the game. His performance prompted E W Swanton to comment: "By any standards he was outstanding, with the superb wrist and eye of the finest...athletes and, what is less common, a calm temper...capable of stemming misfortune. In the Lord's Test only Headley rose to real heights", (even though Cyril Walters and Les Ames had scored more runs).

An unbeaten century from Headley in the second Test at Old Trafford, and a partnership of 200 in 205 minutes with Ivan Barrow ensured the tourists their highest

Test score in England and a draw. They performed admirably despite being subject to 'bodyline' bowling and it was the first occasion they had not lost a Test match by an innings in England. In fine weather the tourists played splendidly for the first three days, with opener, Barrow, reaching his century only a few minutes before Headley, who was batting in his usual position at three. Thus Barrow became the first West Indian to score a Test century in England, although Headley could have reached the landmark first if he had wanted to keep the strike. His performance moved *Wisden* to write: "He cut, drove and forced the ball off his legs to the on with a ready adaptability and perfection of timing which enabled him to resist the English bowling for six-and-a-half hours without giving a single chance." Barrow was finally dismissed for 105, but George went on to 169 not out.

It was a hectic tour for the West Indians. There were only 14 players in the party and Frank Martin injured himself early in the tour which ruled him out of the remaining matches. In addition to playing cricket, George also underwent an operation to have a sebaceous cyst removed from his forehead which had formed after he had fallen from his bicycle as a youngster in Panama. A few days later, as he was convalescing, he heard a newsboy below his hospital window shouting, "Extra! Extra! Cloudburst in Jamaica. George Headley's aunt is among the casualties." He jumped from his bed and sent for the newspaper, which confirmed what he

❑ *Yorkshire's Hedley Verity, who engaged in a battle of wits with the other Headley.*

had heard. His aunt, who had been like a mother to him since he was ten years old, had been drowned in the floods in Kingston. The torrential downpour had rocked the delicate foundations of the Roberts' house and she was washed away with it. In addition, all of George's personal belongings, including his trophies, were lost.

There was no possibility that George would be able to attend the funeral and he returned to his cricket to try and take his mind off the dreadful news. The next match was against Sussex at Brighton and he went into lunch on seven not out. When he returned to the pavilion, it transpired a lot of mail had arrived for him and he was anxious to read it. But official engagements had to come first and he was obliged to lunch with the Lord Mayor. He had no time to read his letters before play resumed but, a few runs later, he was adjudged LBW. He raced back to the dressing-room to check his post. One of the letters was from George Townsend, whose house had been in front of the Roberts'. He sent George a detailed description of the unhappy events in Jamaica, that at least reassured him of exactly what had happened.

Despite this tragic news, Headley continued to bat as only he knew how. Although he was disappointing in the third and final Test at The Oval - making just nine and 12 as West Indies were comprehensively beaten - he topped the batting in the Test series with 277 runs (55.40). Of the other batsmen, only Barrow, Roach and Constantine in the second Test and Roach again, with 56 in the third, made substantial contributions. Of the bowlers, Manny Martindale enjoyed a wonderful debut, collecting 14 wickets (17.92) in the Test series, and thus carried the bowling in much the same way Headley did the batting. Altogether, Headley scored 2,320 runs on the tour (1,000 more than any other West Indian batsman), with seven hundreds, and was third in the first-class averages behind Wally Hammond - although Headley had a better Test series than the Englishman - and Phil Mead. His aggregate was boosted by the 182 he scored against Warwickshire at Birmingham, as he shared in a record fifth wicket partnership of 228 with Cyril Merry, who made 146; and unbeaten double centuries against Somerset and Derbyshire. *Wisden* enthused about the former: "Headley showed his finest form for the West Indies, putting together his third and highest three figure innings of the tour. He scored his 224 out of 440 in five and three-quarter hours without mistake, hitting 31 fours, and remaining undefeated when the innings was declared."

Ivan Barrow was third in the Test averages, after Headley and Constantine, with just under 24. Speaking many years later about George's form before the tour, Barrow recalled: "I always seem to remember him flicking the ball off his pad...most bowlers seemed to be trying to hit his pad, and he was always flicking them past mid-on. Two other features of his batting were that he played the ball late, and that, even when he was attacking, he did so from the crease. I would say, though, that Headley was not at his peak in Australia. He reached that on the England tour of 1933."

The Jamaican's batting in 1933 earned him the honour of being selected as one of *Wisden's* five Cricketers of the Year. Sydney Southerton was clearly impressed: "In all his innings Headley exhibited a sound defence and at the same time very remarkable stroke-play. He was a fine cutter but the outstanding feature of his methods was his powerful and well-placed driving, in which he very often went back on his right leg and forced the ball away at the last possible moment. Difficult to get rid of, he became a dangerous man when well set."

Altogether, it had been a memorable tour for Headley, with the Jamaican one of the few to enhance his reputation. For good measure, his testing spin bowling brought him 21 wickets (34.33), while his fielding also received acclaim. J G Coates observed him at first slip: "It is a pleasure to watch him field, to see him anticipate a stroke, dash for a ball like lightning, pick up at full speed and send the ball hurtling through the arc straight and true to the wicket. He has all the natural grace and unerring accuracy of genius and it is a brave if not a reckless batsman who would dare to steal a single when Headley is fielding the ball."

Again, it was left to *Wisden* to sum up his contribution to that long, hot summer: "From what we had been told by English players who had been to the West Indies we were fully prepared for Headley's success, but even so he astonished most of us..."

Always a great patriot, an enjoyable first visit to England was made extra special when the West Indies captain, Jackie Grant, whose real name was George Copeland Grant, introduced the Jamaican to King George V, who apparently remarked: "Here are three Georges together!" The English public were to see a lot more of George in the coming years as, during the Manchester Test, he signed to play for Haslingden in the Lancashire League in 1934 and 1935 for £500 a season, a reasonable fee which, with collections, would be considerably enhanced.

❏ *Headley and Constantine are pictured here together, but they were on different sides when they thrilled northern crowds during their glory days in the Lancashire League.*

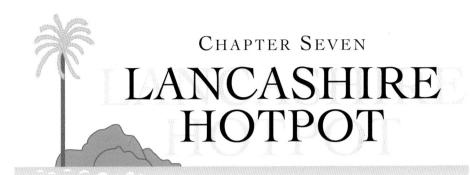

LANCASHIRE HOTPOT

I N 1934 George arrived in England for his first season of Lancashire League cricket. There is a tradition of attacking batting and sporting declarations in the League which makes them popular occasions, while the appearance of Headley further boosted the crowds.

Most clubs hire one professional cricketer and Headley was contracted to play for Haslingden. There was a great sense of anticipation in the northern leagues given Headley's reputation and the performances already achieved in the North by George's Test colleague, Learie Constantine. The most eagerly awaited fixture of the season was billed as 'Haslingden with Headley versus Nelson with Constantine'.

The Trinidadian's brilliant all-round performances on West Indies' tour of England in 1928 prompted a spate of offers from clubs in the Lancashire League, and George's 169 not out in the second Test at Old Trafford five years later brought a similar response.

Haslingden's offer was the highest, and about twice as much as he was earning as a fruit selector with the United Fruit Company. Before accepting, George liaised with the Jamaican Cricket Board, who advised him to sign the contract.

On his second visit to England, George was largely on his own. The first time he had his team mates to relate to and room with, but in Haslingden he found himself practically the only black man in a town of 40,000 people! He encountered a predictable degree of prejudice from the more conservative elements (who would make condescending remarks in his presence, which he would ignore or laugh off) but, generally, the welcome was warm and the people with whom he boarded and the members and supporters of the club quickly took him to their hearts.

Much of the prejudice he experienced was innocuous rather than sinister, such as when a young child who saw George on the street called to his mother, "Mummy, look at a black man!" She quickly quietened the child, explaining, "Oh no, dear. That's Mr Headley, our professional cricketer."

The first match of the season was between Haslingden and Nelson, and George and Learie met up before the start to reminisce on previous games they had played together. On that occasion, however, they were to be on opposing sides. Nelson batted first on a typically bleak Lancashire day. George received his first surprise when he was invited to open the bowling; as a spinner he was used to waiting until some of the shine had gone from the ball. But the captain explained it was the custom for the professional to bowl first; as was also the custom, Nelson gave Haslingden a chance by declaring on 170 for eight, after Constantine had been dismissed for a duck. Predictably, George was soon facing his first ball in league cricket, as Constantine accounted for one of Haslingden's openers in the second over. Headley played his first delivery from Constantine short of extra-cover and set off for a single. However, his partner saw the lightning Constantine homing in on the ball, and in panic turned back. George was left stranded, and Constantine did the honours for Nelson.

It was an inauspicious beginning with Haslingden losing by 60 runs but, as ever, Headley was not slow to adapt his game to the requirements of the situation. He changed from bowling off-spin to medium pace, which later brought rich dividends for Haslingden. Jimmy Brierley, one of his team mates, remembered him setting up a single stump to help improve his bowling. It obviously worked as George took 285 wickets (15.83) during his time at Haslingden. After his early set-back with the bat, Headley was soon into his stride and by the end of the season had established a new league record with 1,063 runs (50.62). Indeed, his batting performances for the club earned him a silver cigarette case with the inscription 'To G A Headley, a little memento for scoring 1,000 runs for Haslingden CC in 1934'.

By the end of the summer George had become an integral part of the Lancashire League scene, but he was involved in a nasty incident when he agreed to take part in a benefit match for the Lancashire and England player, Jack Iddon, towards the end of the season. Before play began, Jack introduced the players to each other. When he introduced George to a South African, Jim Blackenburg, the latter refused to shake his hand. It was an embarrassing incident not helped when Blackenburg later approached George and explained, "I am a great admirer of your cricket but where I come from we do not fraternise with you fellows."

It was probably the most blatant attack of racism he suffered, and he would doubtless have been relieved to discover it was not a personal vendetta. Blackenburg had displayed his remarkable intolerance on another occasion to Constantine, who replaced him at Nelson. Needless to say, both Headley and Constantine showed the South African up on and off the field. The Trinidadian told George how he retaliated: "I beat him, I beat him and when I thought he had had enough, I take my slow ball and I bowl he down."

Headley and Constantine were the first West Indians to appear in the Lancashire League and they were unqualified successes, which meant subsequent players had a lot to live up to. George's contract was renewed every two years and when he asked to be allowed to play for the West Indies during their 1939 tour of England, Haslingden offered him a two year contract covering 1938 and 1940 instead.

By 1935 Manny Martindale had joined Headley and Constantine in the League, by signing for Burnley. George enjoyed one of his finest moments in 1937 against the West Indian newcomer's team. Burnley began well enough scoring over 200, with George bowling for two-and-a-half hours. Clearly the only way Haslingden would overhaul that score was if George opened the batting. He obliged, hammering the fast bowlers as he raced to 122 not out and brought his side victory with seven wickets and 15 minutes to spare. Another memorable performance came the following year when he scored 189 not out in the Worsley Cup, played over five evenings.

In five seasons with Haslingden, George scored 4,957 league runs, with nine centuries, including a top-score of 162 not out, and 33 fifties. His habit of bowling to a single stump improved his bowling sufficiently to take 264 wickets, including five in an innings on 16 occasions. In 1937 he broke the Lancashire League record for most runs in a season when he scored 1,360, with five centuries, which remained a record until Everton Weekes overhauled it by exactly 100 runs in 1949.

❏ *Manny Martindale, who followed in the footsteps of Constantine and Headley by becoming a favourite with the Lancashire League crowds.*

❏ *Derek Sealy, who played a crucial role in West Indies' historic victory at Kingston.*

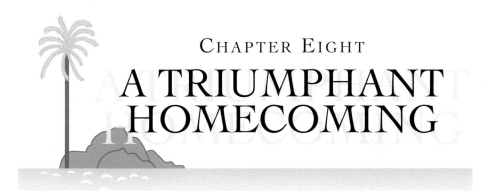

CHAPTER EIGHT
A TRIUMPHANT HOMECOMING

G EORGE returned home from Haslingden to prepare for MCC's second visit early in 1935. This time the tourists did not make the mistake of sending an understrength team. Captained by Bob Wyatt, the England team included such stars as Wally Hammond, Les Ames, Errol Holmes, Jack Iddon, Eric Hollies, George Paine, Maurice Leyland, Jim Smith and Ken Farnes.

Against this glittering line-up the West Indies had many stars of their own: in the fast bowling department Manny Martindale and Leslie Hylton, Puss Achong was their slow bowler, Cyril Christiani their wicket-keeper-batsman, Derek Sealy was now back in the side; Rolph Grant, along with George Carew and Charles Jones were making their debuts, with Clifford Roach the veteran batsman, and Jackie Grant the veteran (by West Indian standards) captain and, of course, 'Mass' George.

In 1935 the West Indies Test team was not so heavily populated by members of the host island, with a more professional attitude towards selecting the teams now holding sway. Whereas in 1930 Barbados had five representatives in the Test played there, it now had three; and there was a similar decline in the case of every other territory - Trinidad from eight to five, British Guiana from seven to four and Jamaica from eight to six.

The English must have felt at home for the first Test at Bridgetown, as rain greeted the players rather than the usual glaring sunshine. The conditions meant that the wicket was virtually unplayable, and the match degenerated into a game of Russian roulette as each side declared successively in an effort to try and avoid the worst of the pitch. Headley showed he was in a class of his own by scoring 44 in West Indies' first innings total of 102 before he was run out, with Hylton's 15 being the next best score. In reply, England made 81 for five before the close of play. An overnight deluge meant that play did not begin on the second day until after tea.

On the resumption Hylton took the wickets of Hammond and Holmes without addition to the score, prompting Wyatt to declare still 21 runs adrift of West Indies' total. In response, Grant juggled his batting order and sent in his fast bowlers to open the innings in an attempt to save his better batsmen until conditions improved. It was a ploy that backfired, as three were dismissed without scoring and West Indies finished the day on 33 for three, with Hylton on 17 not out and 10 extras. In the end, after Headley had confirmed that the wicket was unplayable by getting a duck, Grant declared on 51 for six. England finished on top in this lottery when Hammond struck Martindale - who had taken five wickets in the innings - for six over extra-cover to settle the issue.

The loss of the match at Bridgetown seemed to inspire the West Indians to play with added resolve at Port-of Spain, as the defeat in Trinidad in 1930 had inspired them at Georgetown. The availability of Constantine immediately strengthened West Indies' hand and they made 302 in their first innings, with Constantine scoring a hard-hit 90 and Sealy 92; George made 25. They then bowled out the English for 258, whereupon West Indies' openers were dismissed cheaply for the second time in the match. However, George was soon making amends and by the close of play had scored 69 out of West Indies' total of 150. The next morning he decided attack was the best form of defence and dispatched several balls to the boundary, before being adjudged LBW to Jim Smith when on 93, the only time he was dismissed in the nineties in his Test career. Despite the disappointment of missing out on his century, two smart catches in the slips by Headley helped the West Indies to secure victory, as Constantine and Hylton did the damage with the ball.

MCC adopted more defensive tactics in the rain-affected third Test at Georgetown. Headley top-scored with 53 out of 184 batting at four, and did not bat in the second innings as the game headed to a draw.

The teams arrived in Kingston with the series level and West Indies confident that with George leading their batting - he had recently made 127 for Jamaica against the tourists at Melbourne Park - and Martindale, Constantine and Hylton taking care of the bowling they could clinch the rubber. West Indies batted first and found the English bowling very accurate, and it took the application of Headley to lift the scoring rate. Slowly, but surely, in partnership with Derek Sealy the pair got on top of the bowling, and went on to a record third wicket partnership of 202. Eventually the young Barbadian was dismissed for 97 and George then continued with Rolph Grant, as the pair shared in a seventh wicket partnership of 147, before Grant was dismissed for 77. However, the English seemed powerless to stop Headley: the nagging length of Hollies could not frustrate him, the pace of Smith and Farnes was dispatched to the boundary whenever it was loose, while the leg-breaks of Paine received equally harsh treatment. When the West Indies finally declared on their highest Test score of 535 for seven, George was still unbeaten on 270 after eight hours of batting, having hit 30 fours to establish the highest score against England by a West Indian until Lawrence Rowe's 302 in 1974.

The West Indian bowlers were inspired by his innings and proceeded to dismiss the visitors for 271, with Martindale and Constantine doing most of the damage. Their performance prompted the home side to enforce the follow-on. MCC were without their captain, Wyatt, whose jaw had been fractured by Martindale in the first innings. The final day was played under overcast skies and the fear that rain might prevent an outright result. Things seemed to be going well for the home side until Grant sprained his ankle and had to leave the field. Constantine took over the captaincy and immediately introduced Sealy into the attack so he could swop ends with Martindale. Sealy obligingly took a wicket, before the two frontline bowlers completed the job, as West Indies won by an innings and 161 runs, and so secured their first-ever victory in

❑ *Bob Wyatt, MCC captain in 1934-35.*

a Test series. Headley had scored 485 runs in the rubber for an average of 97 - more than double his nearest rival - and had made the highest score by either side in all but the third Test, when his score was only beaten by Wyatt's 71.

As the players left the field, a light drizzle start to fall. Errol Holmes who congratulated the West Indies in the absence of Wyatt added wryly, "I see that the rain has just been a little bit too late for us!" Then, the Jamaican crowd called for their heroes: Martindale and Constantine and, of course, their own son, 'Mass' George, whose success brought celebration among the West Indians in Colon, Panama, as well and the following comments from the *Daily Gleaner*: "The chief honour in this glorious victory belongs to Headley; without his indomitable batting we would never have brought this match to a finish...He deserves well of his country and if this were a place where men with some of this world's wealth abounded, I am quite sure he would be amply provided for, instead of having to work for a living abroad."

George did not have another opportunity to excel against an English attack in a Test match until 1939, but in 1936 Yorkshire, the English county champions, toured Jamaica under the leadership of Paul Gibb. The tour party boasted such names as Hedley Verity, Bill Bowes and Herbert Sutcliffe, but they played dour cricket, being defensive in their batting and bowling. In a dull series, George scored 266 runs from five innings, with one century, for an average of 53.20.

It was during this series that George had his first dispute with the Jamaican Cricket Board about how he should be treated as a professional. He had played in the trial matches, captaining one of the sides without asking for payment. However the Board paid for the expenses of the Yorkshiremen, including their passage from England and hotel fees, which prompted George to approach the Secretary of the Board and point out that he, too, was a professional cricketer and would like to be financially reimbursed for his efforts. His request met with a cool response, "Surely, George, you are not going to charge us a fee...you learnt your cricket here." But Headley persisted, pointing out that he now earned his living by playing cricket. His request was put before the Board and the day before the final match, he was informed that his fees had been approved.

□ **West Indies touring party to England, May 1939.**

Standing (l-r): Gerry Gomez, Bertie Clarke, Jeff Stollmeyer, Tyrell Johnson, Philip Bayley, Ken Weekes, 'Foffie' Williams, Leslie Hylton, John Cameron.

Sitting (l-r): Manny Martindale, George Headley, Jack Kidney, Rolph Grant, Learie Constantine, Ivan Barrow, Derek Sealy.

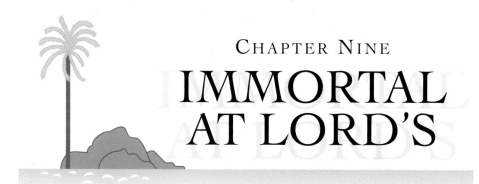

CHAPTER NINE

IMMORTAL
AT LORD'S

EORGE HEADLEY had a splendid series in England in 1939 and could not have known that he would never take part in a full Test series again. He arrived in England with a reputation as one of the top batsmen in the world: he had not failed in any of his Test series and had played outstandingly well in all conditions (indeed his standing in Jamaica, where he had scored thousands of runs in domestic cricket, was such that if the opposition got less than 200, the locals would boast, "Not to worry, 'Mass' George will knock those off by himself.") In addition, Headley had eight Test hundreds to his credit, made a triple century in first-class cricket and shared in a world record partnership. He had also achieved the rare distinction of scoring 1,000 runs in an Australian first-class season and 2,000 in an English one. But again, like his colleague Constantine, George had been passed over for the captaincy.

Headley's performance in the Lord's Test of 1939, when he scored a century in each innings, was the high point of his glittering career. It made him one of cricket's greatest 'immortals': he had already scored a century in each innings of the Georgetown Test of 1930; but to have achieved the feat at the home of cricket put him in a class of his own. For the people of Jamaica, it was his ultimate triumph and they cherished him as a champion, their champion: a black man made good against all the odds.

The West Indies hadn't played a Test series for four years, but George had learned much in league cricket. At 30 years old, most people believed Headley was at his peak. England might have known they were in for a tough time: captaining Jamaica in the trial matches in Trinidad, he scored 160 and 103. It was an ominous sign. Again England could field a strong side, captained by Wally Hammond and including the likes of Harold Gimblett, Eddie Paynter, Joe Hardstaff, Arthur Fagg and newcomers, Len Hutton and Denis Compton in the batting department, and Tom Goddard, Bill Copson, Doug Wright, Hedley Verity, Ken Farnes and Bill Bowes in the bowling.

The West Indies had Rolph Grant, brother of Jackie, as their captain as well as the talent of Constantine, Martindale, Hylton, Sealy and Barrow, while Jeff Stollmeyer and Gerry Gomez of Trinidad, Bertie Clarke of Barbados and John Cameron of Jamaica, were making their international debuts, alongside George's Lucas club mate, Ken Weekes.

Headley invariably dominated the West Indian innings in the county matches, as when he scored 164 without being dismissed out of 353 against Essex at Chelmsford, while 13 wickets for 91 from Constantine ensured victory for the tourists. In the next match against Middlesex at Lord's Headley completed his third hundred and first double hundred of the tour as West Indies amassed 665, to warm-up for the first Test at the St John's Wood ground.

As so often, George had slept little on the eve of the Test preferring to go over the match in his mind and anticipate the likely tactics of the opposition. C L R James elaborates: "But he isn't suffering from insomnia, not in the least. This fantastic man is busy playing his innings the next day. The fast bowler will swing from leg. He plays a stroke. Then the bowler will come in from the off. He plays the stroke to correspond. The bowler will shorten. George hooks or cuts. Verity will keep a length on or just outside the off-stump. George will force him away by getting back to cut and must be on guard not to go too greedily at a loose ball - that is how in Tests he most fears he will lose his innings (a revealing commentary on his attitude to bowlers). Langridge will flight the ball. Down the pitch to drive. So he goes through every conceivable ball and makes a stroke to correspond."

As a result of this mental preparation George arrived at the ground completely relaxed and ready to take what lay ahead in his stride. West Indies won the toss and batted. Grant and Stollmeyer put on just 29, before Grant fell to Copson.

Headley began cautiously, slowing getting into his stride as he nurtured the 18-year-old Stollmeyer at the other end. His approach paid rich dividends, as the pair added 118 before the debutant was clean bowled by Bowes. After that, West Indies' batting looked precarious which meant that George had to farm the bowling. Despite poor light and testing bowling, Headley helped himself to a chanceless century. He was finally caught behind for 106, as the visitors totalled 277. The West Indies bowled well enough when England first came into bat, collecting three

❏ *Lording it at the Mecca of cricket...*

relatively cheap wickets. But then Hutton and Compton made hundreds to help England to top 400 runs before they declared.

On the Saturday morning Lord's was bathed in bright sunshine, which would have pleased the 12,000 strong crowd. Less pleasing from a West Indian point of view was the early dismissal of Stollmeyer. Once again Headley found himself opening the innings to all intents and purposes, and realised that he would have to bat for a long time to ensure a draw. He began cautiously taking two hours for his first 50, partnered by Derek Sealy, who had stayed at the wicket with him in the past. But then Sealy was dismissed and Ken Weekes removed after a bright 16, which made Headley realise the importance of re-applying himself. Once more he found himself looking for a single off the last ball of the over in the face of tight fielding from the Englishmen.

When he reached 72, he passed 1,000 runs for the tour, and as he crept toward the nineties, cricketing pundits were aware that history was in the making (it was therefore especially fitting that it was the first time the BBC were transmitting ball-by-ball commentary). If he reached his second century of the match, he would be the first player to achieve this feat at Lord's, and having already reached this landmark at Georgetown nine years earlier, he would join Herbert Sutcliffe as the only other player to do it on two occasions.

As batsmen at the other end fell to the guile of Verity and Wright, Headley stuck to his task. He moved to 97, with West Indies' total on 199 and every spectator in the

... and in both cases wicket-keeper, Arthur Wood, was the helpless spectator.

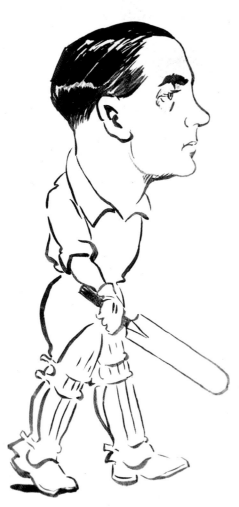

❏ Herbert Sutcliffe, who was the only player before Headley to score two hundreds in a Test match twice.

ground searching for the best view. Then a short-pitched ball from Wright settled the issue as George crashed it past square-leg. Even before it struck the boundary the applause began, resounding louder and louder in acknowledgement of a great sporting moment.

When the excitement died down Headley returned to his task, anxious to keep his partner away from the probing English attack. He had scored 107 and was preparing to take a run off Wright, in order to face Verity, when Hammond brought his fielders in. Those tactics left George in two minds about how to play the last delivery and he ended up knocking a catch to Hutton. On his way back to the pavilion, the Jamaican received a standing ovation and the hearty congratulations of his team mates in the dressing-room. An historic day was made complete when Sir Pelham Warner arrived to add his good wishes. In recognition of his unique achievement, Headley was presented with two silver serving dishes inscribed with his respective scores of 106 and 107. Indeed, it was a memorable week for George as his wife, Rena, gave birth to a son two days after the Lord's Test. He was christened Ron, and was the only one of George's nine children brave enough to follow in his father's foot-steps and take up cricket as a career.

'At the end of the 1939 West Indian tour, E W Swanton was moved to write: "They were not a formidable side, depending unduly on the great George Headley in batting...at Lord's in the first Test they were out-played. Hutton made 196, batting as if there had been no break since his last home Test innings at the Oval (his world record 364), and Compton played beautifully for 120; but, even so, chief honours went to Headley who, with 106 and 107, made history by being the one and only man to score two hundreds in a Test at Lord's". It wasn't until 1990 that this feat was emulated again at Lord's, when Graham Gooch scored 333 and 123 against India.

❏ C B Fry, the great English batsman turned commentator, who gave Headley the famous nickname of 'Atlas' in recognition of his shouldering of West Indies batting.

1939, a Vintage
Year for George

*In full flow against England
(above and Surrey below)...*

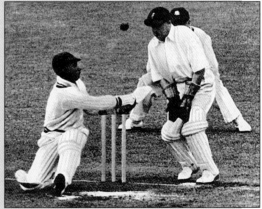

... and against Middlesex (above).

As that was Headley's first Test since his unbeaten double century at Sabina Park in 1935 he had scored three hundreds in his last three Test innings. At that time only Jack Fingleton had beaten this record with four centuries in consecutive innings and only Herbert Sutcliffe, Warren Bardsley and Charles Macartney had equalled the feat.

C B Fry, the great pre-1914 English batsman turned prominent sports writer, commented: "His middle name should be 'Atlas'" (after the mythological figure who held up the world on his shoulders); it was a title that stuck - with many pictures of him at that time captioned by that word alone - and his performance in the Lord's Test had done more than anything else to earn him that accolade.

Despite his own personal triumph - he scored over a third of West Indies' runs - George was displeased that West Indies had lost the match. In the end, England were set 99 to win, a target they reached with eight wickets to spare. Even though, on paper, it seemed a comprehensive victory they made the runs with only a few minutes to spare. However, besides his own performance, Headley was impressed with Weekes' century and in a rare interview was finally persuaded to comment on his own innings: "My two centuries at Lord's were defensive rather than attacking. We were facing defeat, and I tried to avert this by staying at the wicket and scoring whenever possible, rather than trying to take the bowling by the scruff of the neck. I wasn't deliberately trying to become an 'Immortal'. Indeed, at the time I don't recall being elated - it was just one of those things which happen in a man's life. My immediate reaction was one of disappointment that I hadn't been able to prevent us losing, rather than any sense of joy at what I had achieved."

West Indies' next county match, against Nottinghamshire, produced the second double hundred of the season for Headley, 234 out of a total of 510 for three declared. He distinguished himself again with the bat, when he played a magnificent innings of 61 on a 'sticky dog' wicket against Yorkshire and the tenacious bowling of Hedley Verity. Indeed, his performance on that day prompted Neville Cardus to describe it as one of the finest innings he had ever witnessed.

The second Test at Old Trafford was played in bleak conditions. England won the toss and batted first, declaring on 164 for seven. In reply West Indies made 133, with George top-scoring with 51 before he was the last man out, and thereby became the first West Indian to score 50 in six consecutive Test innings. Martindale and Constantine then produced their best form of the series, snapping up six English wickets between them before the home side declared leaving West Indies to score 160 runs to win in 70 minutes. It was an impossible task and the visitors finished on 43 for four.

West Indies went to The Oval, needing victory to level the series. Despite enjoying a good batting wicket, the English were restricted to 352 in their first innings thanks to more splendid bowling from Constantine and some top-class fielding. They maintained their good form when it was their turn to bat, rattling up 498 in quick time. George scored 65 and seemed to be heading for yet another century, but a mix-up with debutant Vic Stollmeyer ended with George being run out. The older Stollmeyer atoned for the misunderstanding with a fine 96 and apologised to George when he returned to the pavilion, but the master made light of it. The Press, however, were not so forgiving, although a splendid century from Ken Weekes, greatly admired by George, soon diverted attention from the unfortunate Stollmeyer. Lord

Tennyson was one of the enthusiastic spectators that day. However, time was ticking over and some fine second innings batting from England, more worthy of the nature of the pitch, helped the home side to 366 for three and ensured that the game was drawn.

Headley had scored 1,745 runs, with six centuries and eight half-centuries, from his 30 first-class innings in England which helped him to top the national averages with 72.70 In a wet summer, the next player was Hammond, with an average of 63.56. In the Tests Headley averaged 66.80, the next was Ken Weekes with 57.66, but of his total of 173 he made 137 in one innings. The next man (Constantine) averaged 27.50.

The Jamaican's batting had won him widespread acclaim. Sir Pelham Warner wrote: "He bats very naturally and very easily, and ranks in that very small class of stylists which includes Hobbs, Woolley, Kippax and Hammond."

R C Robertson-Glasgow paid this tribute: "He delights in hooking, in delaying deflections to leg, and in cutting square or late. In these arts he has no living superior. Great batting often has the beauty of blast or the grandeur of the gale. In Headley's art there is no noise. But it answers the test of greatness. As he walks down the pavilion steps you expect, hope or fear."

It was Neville Cardus who first somewhat controversially referred to Headley as the 'Black Bradman' at a farewell lunch for the departing West Indian team at the Savoy Hotel, and later in his speech referred to him as "the greatest living cricketer of our generation". The sports commentator, Denzil Batchelor, was equally explicit: "There are times when I think that the Don at his very best was fit to be called the white Headley." Learie Constantine, writing at a later date, wisely declined to make a comparison contenting himself with the remark, "Two centuries in a Test is a feat very rarely accomplished, and George was the first player ever to do so at Lord's. He had long been recognised as one of the two best batsmen in the world."

Robertson-Glasgow in the 1939 *Wisden* wrote: "No mathematics can recapture George Headley batting v England at Lord's in the first Test, looking far smaller out there than the 140 odd pounds of weight that he claims, quietly defiant, artistic in cutting, watchful in the line of the ball in defence...Some criticised his style of playing so many strokes off the back foot, and it is true that no batsman, however great, looks so well playing like that...but he showed himself to have no living superior in the square and the late cut. He was wonderful, too, in hooking and in that very late flick of the ball from thigh or hips to long leg. I can see a resemblance to Bradman in his strokes, like Bradman, too, he seems to play the ball very late yet with certainty."

But if George's personal world was bright and full of hope, the outside world was less promising. War clouds were looming over Europe and the last seven games of the tour were cancelled as the tourists were advised to return home. In fact they reached Montreal on 3 September, the Sunday that Britain declared war on Germany.

CHAPTER TEN
A WAITING GAME

HE SECOND WORLD WAR had a profound effect on Headley's career. There is no telling what sort of records he could have set during those years. As it was, for various reasons, he only played in three post-War Tests, while his great rivals, Don Bradman and Wally Hammond were to play 15 and eight respectively, even though they were older. Ironically George's final Test appearance came six years after Bradman had retired and seven after Hammond's departure from the international scene. But his failure to gain selection could not have been a question of loss of form as, 19 years after his 211 for a Jamaican XI against Lord Tennyson's side in 1928, George batted for 203 not out against a strong Barbadian side.

He had been due to return to Haslingden in 1940 but professionals were not employed by the Lancashire League during the War so he remained in Jamaica. He began working for the Jamaican government at the Labour Department, which later became the Ministry of Labour, and played for Lucas CC in the Senior Cup, captaining the side in 1940, 1941 and 1944. They were always in contention for the Senior Cup with George the mainstay of the batting. He scored 786 runs in 1940, 638 in 1943 and 830 in 1944. Indeed, Lucas enjoyed so much success during those years - winning the Cup in 1940, 1941 and 1944 - that it was looked on as a golden age.

Meanwhile, a great wealth of cricketing talent was emerging in the islands of the Eastern Caribbean, aided by the 'Goodwill Tournaments' played by Barbados, Trinidad and British Guiana. The leading lights of this new batch of cricketers were headed by the three 'W's: Frank Worrell, Clyde Walcott and Everton Weekes.

In 1945 Headley had his first taste of international competition for six years when he made a short visit to America for a series of exhibition matches. The Jamaican was accompanied by John Holt Jnr and it was a splendid learning experience for the youngster in much the same way as Headley's visit with John Holt Snr to America way back in 1929 had enhanced his game; Worrell was another of the West Indian rising stars who went as well.

Jamaica's isolation from the first-class scene ended when Trinidad became the first team to fly to the island for a three match series in June 1946. The relative inactivity of the War years had taken its toll on Headley, who was not in the best of

❑ *The three 'W's, Frank Worrell, Clyde Walcott and Everton Weekes, whose batting was to take the Caribbean domestic competitions and Test arena by storm in the post-war years.*

health. During the three matches he had one good innings of 99 in the last game. However, he bowled in these games and was the leading wicket-taker for Jamaica.

A huge crowd turned out for the first match at Sabina Park. Trinidad, captained by Jeff Stollmeyer, batted first and collapsed to 159 all out after incisive bowling from Hines Johnson and Dickie Fuller. When Jamaica batted, George appeared to be playing with his usual fluency, before he was bowled by Derek Sealy. Thereafter Ken Weekes and J K Holt Jnr shared in a superb century stand that delighted the home crowd, while more splendid batting from Rickards helped Jamaica to 280. Trinidad put up a much better showing in their second innings and, after losing one of their openers early on, consolidated their position to reach 40 without loss. It was at that stage that Jamaica's captain, Cecil Marley, decided to bring on George who had won something of a reputation as a bowler in English league cricket and also bowled as captain of Lucas.

He had the opposition in trouble from the moment he took the ball: a misjudgement from Rupert Tang Choon helped him to a wicket-maiden in his first over, before bowling Andy Ganteaume in his second. So far, no one had scored off his bowling. The crowd waited in hushed expectation as Prior Jones made his way to the wicket. George didn't disappoint them as he bowled the Trinidadian paceman with his second ball to give him three wickets for no runs from 14 balls! His success prompted an over-excited crowd to invade the pitch and, with just five minutes to go, play was abandoned for the day with Trinidad on a vulnerable 40 for four. The next day the visitors were bowled out for 150, as Jamaica won by eight wickets, and George returned bowling figures of five for 33.

During that match Marley had been injured, so George captained Jamaica for the rest of the series. He had a wealth of experience to draw on and performed admirably. At the end of the tournament one sports commentator wrote: "George Headley handled his bowling splendidly; his bringing in of two bowlers unknown to Trinidad, young Holt and Rickards, for an over or two, just to break the sequence of the regulars, having an electric effect. Holt got a good wicket, and Rickards had chances missed off him, after which, George resumed with his regulars..."

At the end of the series there was an official function where the players were awarded prizes for the performances. George was presented with a watch for making the best all-round contribution in the series by the Governor, Sir John Huggins, and also won a bat donated by Wally Hammond for making the highest score (his 99 in the last match) of the series. As a bonus, he received a subscription from 'Crab' Nethersole collected for him during the competition. Nethersole, who was then a councillor, remarked: "One of the happy events of this tour has been the revival of widespread interest in cricket, and one of the most pleasant duties that have fallen to us is for those of us who have taken pleasure in his performances to assist in making up a subscription for George Headley." In his acceptance speech, George stated: "I am very grateful indeed to those who willingly subscribed to my benefit and I need hardly mention that the Trinidadian team, our visitors, throughout the series of matches, played cricket in a way which not only the All Jamaica representatives but the public thoroughly enjoyed. I sincerely hope that in the near future Jamaica will find it convenient to return this visit. To Mr Jeffrey Stollmeyer and his team, I wish good luck."

Soon afterwards George made a visit to New York for a series of matches. The invitation came from U C Durrant, who was keen to make sure the expatriate West Indian community there maintained their interest. Of the up-and-coming players, Ken Weekes, J K Holt, Frank Worrell and Everton Weekes were also invited, and this is where George first became well acquainted with the play of Worrell and Weekes.

After the success of the series against Trinidad, the Jamaican Board was keen to set a precedent of inviting teams from the Eastern Caribbean to tour the island and in 1947 duly extended an invitation to Barbados. They also took the important step of appointing George as captain of Jamaica in his own right, rather than vice-captain. It was at this time that George approached the Jamaican Board about providing a transport and kit allowance for those who were on a low income. Despite their initial misgivings, it was the first step towards concern for the welfare of first-class cricketers.

Although the English had brought the game to the West Indies, it was now clear that many black cricketers had acquired sufficient knowledge and skill to take over the leadership of their teams. Indeed, on many occasions, it was apparent that several of the black players were more talented than their white counterparts. Even so, in many influential quarters, the view persisted that only men of European appearance were suitable to lead teams, so Jamaica's stance in appointing George as captain was of historic significance.

The old colonial attitude was revealed most blatantly when Learie Constantine was overlooked for the captaincy to Australia in 1930-31, as the selectors preferred to put their faith in Jackie Grant, who had never captained a side before let alone played Test cricket. Even so, there was progress of a sort. Learie and George were no longer obliged to share a bed as they had done during the Test match in British Guiana in

1930. In Australia George found himself rooming with the white, amateur captain. Indeed, the pair often used to pray together, perhaps for an end to prejudice!

George had, in fact, captained Jamaica as far back as 1939. He led the side during the trial matches for choosing the West Indies team to tour England that year. These games were held in Trinidad as it was felt that the matting wickets there were the closest to the ones the visitors could expect to find in England. 'Crab' Nethersole had originally been appointed manager and captain of the Jamaican team bound for Trinidad, but he had recently been elected First Vice-President of the newly-founded People's National Party, and had decided to opt out of the tour in the interests of his political career, and invited George to skipper the side in his absence. George accepted and distinguished himself with 160 against Trinidad and 93 against a combined side, being ably supported by his protégé, Ken Weekes.

The Second World War brought about many changes, not least a

❏ *Ken Weekes, one of Headley's protégés.*

72

❏ *Posing for the camera. In the post-war era, George had to adopt a diplomatic pose as he watched less talented white players being handed the captaincy of the West Indies.*

feeling of nationalism in the colonies and a desire for self-government. Colonial soldiers had been called on to throw off the yoke of Hitler's domination of Europe, now it was time for the Allies, including Britain, to put her house in order.

Errol Edwards, a friend of Headley's from the 1930's, recalls: "All the captains of Jamaica until George used to be white or nearly white, but they all looked to him for advice: his cricket brain was second to none. It wasn't until after the War that he got his due recognition and was appointed captain of West Indies. Then when he was injured and did not play in the final match in Jamaica, John Goddard, who had replaced him, sent notes to George throughout the Test asking for his advice. In those days you had to take those sort of injustices in your stride, or you got nowhere. George should have come with the 1928 side to England, but others with less ability, who came from the right families and played for the right clubs, were selected in front of him."

Headley's appointment as captain of Jamaica in 1947 was relatively clear-cut: he was so overwhelmingly the best candidate for the job it would have been impossible

❏ *Jeff Stollmeyer and Allan Rae, the first of many famous opening partnerships for the West Indies. Both men had good reason to be grateful for the words of praise and encouragement offered from Headley. Stollmeyer, in particular, benefited from his advice on captaincy.*

to overlook him. As in all aspects of his life he was meticulous in his preparation and supervised the Jamaican practice sessions and also studied in great detail the strengths and weaknesses of his Barbadian opponents. In addition, he had observed the three 'W's on the tours of the US and his homework soon paid off: in the second match of the inter-colonial tournament, between Jamaica and Barbados, he induced Everton Weekes, who was on 97, to snick a catch to George Mudie and caught and bowled Clyde Walcott for 16, while Worrell was run out. For good measure, Headley also took the wickets of Norman Marshall and H L V Griffith, to finish with four for 40. In the end, Barbados scored 325 and Jamaica went into bat in overcast conditions. As so often, Headley had barely finished buckling his pads before the first wicket fell.

As the other opener, Dujon, seemed somewhat unsteady, George decided to farm the bowling. He met with great success playing the good balls carefully and dispatching the bad ones to the boundary and by the end of the day was unbeaten on 64 out of a Jamaican total of 147 for three. A change of bats seemed to bring all the old rhythm back into his game. He had borrowed Arthur McKenzie's bat during a net practice, after he had seen the youngster with a new bat and offered to break it in for him in jest. McKenzie was delighted to oblige, and Headley found the balance so well-suited for his game that McKenzie suggested he keep it for the coming series. George's own bat had a creak and soon after he started his innings with that bat, there was an appeal for a catch behind the wicket. George was sure he hadn't got a touch and decided that the creak might have influenced the fielders. He immediately signalled to the pavilion for another bat and McKenzie sent his out without hesitation.

George batted through the second day, until rain interrupted proceedings, as he took his score from 64 to 183 not out, with the other batsmen contributing just 58. Everyone was ecstatic; one commentator wrote: "He may have played many bigger innings but he has not played a greater." It was the first time Headley had scored a century since his unbeaten innings of 234 against Nottinghamshire at Trent Bridge during West Indies' tour of England in 1939, and confirmed that he had lost none of his powers of concentration.

He continually out-witted the Barbadian captain, John Goddard, who bowled himself, Frank Worrell and Norman Marshall almost to a standstill. The Jamaican would frequently play the first seven deliveries without scoring (eight ball overs had been introduced during the War) and snatch a single from the last ball of the over, only feeling able to play more fluently when he was partnered by the elegant Rickards. At one point Goddard tried to intimidate Headley by placing a fielder at silly mid-off a few yards from his bat, but some hearty blows from George soon brought a change in tactics. Marshall started to bowl wide of the off-stump out of George's reach, but that was a fruitless exercise as, almost at will, the Jamaican would move across his stumps and dispatch it for four. He had reached 97 by lunch and showed uncharacteristic caution in reaching his century. He had been dismissed on 99 the previous year and had got Everton Weekes out in the nineties, and did not want to make a similar mistake. He decided to get the three he needed in singles, and opened his shoulders again once he had reached his hundred.

Whatever tactics Goddard employed and whichever bowler he tried, Headley was equal to them. As C L R James noted he did not care who bowled at him: right hand, left hand, new ball, old ball, slow, fast all were the same. By the time McKenzie came into bat 43 runs were still needed to match Barbados' score of 325; by that stage of the game Headley was monopolising the bowling with clinical precision. By close of play they had added 42 with Headley making 41 of them. The newspapers were once again full of praise. One wrote: "Jamaicans have read, and some have seen, his two great efforts of 107 and 106 for the West Indies against England at Lord's in 1939, but we wonder if they could have been greater."

On the fourth day George moved to his double century. McKenzie was dismissed early on and it was last man, Gooden, who allowed Headley to reach what was to be the last double hundred of his career. The master hooked Worrell for four and then Gooden faced the bowling. But he was not intimidated by the situation and crashed Goddard for six before taking a single to give George the bowling. Headley then got a boundary himself and took a single off the last ball of the over to take him to 199. He reached his double hundred with a majestic cover drive and remained unbeaten on 203 out of a total of 356, as Gooden fell for 11. His innings was the highest by a Jamaican in an inter-colonial match, beating Frank Martin's 195 against the same opponents in Bridgetown in 1925. Headley was cheered off the field, although heavy scoring from Barbados and rain meant the game ended in a draw. George made 57 not out in a total of 151 for five in the second innings, and decided to give McKenzie a new bat in preference to returning his most recent acquisition.

There were some alterations to the Jamaican team for the next match and the selection committee took it upon themselves to present George with the batting order. He did not agree with it entirely and decided to make some alterations. When he informed Karl Nunes, the President of the Jamaican Board the following day, he was sceptical about the plan. But George was happy with his revised batting order and decided to press ahead. He sent Allan Rae and Arthur McKenzie in to open the innings with the instructions that they weren't to return to the dressing room until lunch time. They responded well to his call and shared in an opening stand of 76 before McKenzie was out for 35. George then joined Rae, who went on to score a century as the pair added 148 for the second wicket. Indeed, early on in his innings, George had limited his scoring, as he wanted to make sure his young protégé reached his century before Jamaica totalled 200, when the opposition could have taken the new ball. To confirm the wisdom of George's decision to promote Rae to open the innings, Rae also scored a century in the second innings as a prelude to the success he was to enjoy in that position at Test level.

George, too, was batting well and enjoyed a fruitful partnership with Ken Weekes. When George was on 79, the pair decided on a short single which resulted in George falling and injuring his knee as he struggled to make his ground. The injury ruled him out of the rest of the match and was the first of many that were to dog him for the rest of his career. D P Beckford took over from him and Jamaica finished on 456; but splendid batting from Barbados, in particular Everton Weekes who scored a century, enabled the tourists to gain a first innings lead. However, Rae's second hundred of the match and more superb batting from Ken Weekes ensured a draw.

At the end of the series, there was the usual prize-giving ceremony for best performances. George had played so well that he ended up winning several watches and, appropriately enough and in keeping with his generous nature, he gave one to Rae.

Shortly after the departure of the Barbadians, George received another invitation to play cricket in New York from U C Durrant who wanted him to bring along some other promising players. George took Ken Weekes, J K Holt, Irvine Iffla and Hines Johnson. When the Jamaicans arrived they found that players from the other islands had also been invited, including Prior Jones, Andy Ganteaume and Rupert Tang Choon from Trinidad and the three 'W's from Barbados. This was a sensible move, as it allowed the players from the three islands to become acquainted with each other before the first post-war Test series, due to be played against England in the Caribbean in 1948.

Soon after the American trip George was packing his bags again: this time he was to lead Jamaica in a series against British Guiana in Guiana. In both matches the visitors secured a first innings lead but rain meant the games fizzled into a draw. J K Holt and O J Cunningham made centuries for Jamaica, and Bruce Pairaudeau and Robert Christiani did likewise for Guiana. But, it was an unsatisfactory series for George. He thought the umpires were biased and discovered that the balls were being switched; he also injured his thumb while fielding. Worst of all was the behaviour of the crowd, which must have brought back memories of his unfortunate encounter with Jim Blackenburg in England. Many of the spectators disapproved of a black man leading a team in a first-class match, and booed whenever he changed his bowlers or made alterations to his field.

During the Second World War the question of who should captain the West Indies was put on ice. When George was appointed captain of Jamaica in 1947, most people felt it was the right decision. But, as was seen with his treatment in British Guiana, not everyone held such progressive views. As a result fragmentation returned to the captaincy of the West Indies team during the Test series of 1948. There were to be three captains for that series, with George appointed as skipper for the first Test in Barbados and the final match in Kingston.

George travelled to Barbados for the first Test as the sole representative from Jamaica. On his arrival he was concerned to discover

❏ *John Goddard, who captained West Indies on their first tour of India.*

that Worrell was ill and Walcott injured. Even though Worrell did not recover in time, Walcott was fit enough to open the innings with Stollmeyer. George began promisingly by winning the toss from the MCC captain, Ken Cranston, and elected to bat. When later in the match he led the West Indies on to the field he heard an enthusiastic local shout: "Lordie! Lordie! Look what I live to see, man o' mi own colour leading a West Indies team!"

The pitch at Kensington Oval had been covered overnight and sweated, which helped to account for the wickets of Walcott and Weekes. But by lunch time it had dried out and become more docile allowing Stollmeyer and Gerry Gomez to enjoy a splendid partnership. When Stollmeyer was dismissed for 78, George took his place and West Indies finished the first day on 244 for three. They seemed set for a big score but a sharp shower of rain helped Jim Laker, who took seven for 103 (including the wickets of Gomez for 86 and Headley for 29) and West Indies were all out for 296.

But George marshalled his resources splendidly: the bowlers were penetrative and well-supported by excellent fielding. Even so his toil in the field affected George's back muscles and he had to leave the field limping. But he had set West Indies on their way and the English were bowled out 43 short of the home score. In the second innings West Indies declared on 351 for nine, thanks to fine innings from Christiani and 'Foffie' Williams who scored a dazzling 72 in an hour. George held himself in reserve and finished on seven not out batting at number 10. The tourists went into the final day requiring 335 to win with eight wickets in hand and, at 86 for four, looked decidedly precarious. But then a deluge came down and swamped Kensington Oval, depriving West Indies of a chance of victory.

George travelled to Trinidad as a player awaiting selection because Gomez had already been nominated captain for the second Test. In the nets George found his back pain was hindering his game and he sought medical attention. He could not get satisfactory treatment and asked to be allowed to return home to see his own doctor. The request was granted and he missed the second and third Tests of that series.

George's condition had improved by the time of the two colony matches Jamaica were due to play against MCC. He played in the first game (scoring 65 in his only innings) and then suggested to the Jamaican Board that he should be rested in the second, given his recent back problems and in view of the imminent final Test. However, the Board were not amenable to this idea which they thought would have an adverse effect on gate receipts and he was obliged to play. It was a short-sighted decision, as his back deteriorated and he advised the West Indies Board to omit him from the final Test line-up; Everton Weekes was called up as a replacement and John Goddard took over the captaincy. The West Indies won the Test at Kingston by 10 wickets which prompted the selectors to ignore George and name Goddard as captain for the first tour of India in 1948-49. Indeed, George only made the trip because 'Crab' Nethersole used his influence to make the Labour Department, for whom he was then working, give him the necessary leave.

It proved to be the end of the road for George's captaincy aspirations, but the fact that he had been the first black man to lead the West Indies was a move of profound social and political significance. Indeed, it is inconceivable that, but for his colour, that George would not have captained the side earlier and on many other occasions. Almost without exception, George had played his Test career under men with less appreciation of the finer points of strategy and tactics. However, they did have the vital pre-requisite for a West Indian captain in those days, namely a white skin. In a sense, though, they too were victims of the system, doubtless very conscious of having someone of George's calibre playing under them. However, in keeping with his reserved nature, George was unobtrusive in his support which was always greatly appreciated.

George was invariably complimentary about his colleagues, or preferred to say nothing. When Jeff Stollmeyer retired from first-class cricket three tributes from former West Indian captains appeared in the Press. George was one of those captains, with Karl Nunes and Rolph Grant being the other two. George wrote: "From Stollmeyer's advent into first-class cricket, he has never denied himself the opportunity of improving his knowledge of the game. As a result he became a highly informed student of the game, and a successful cricketer. His contribution to West Indian cricket over the years should be a model to the up-and-coming cricketer."

As a result of these comments, Stollmeyer wrote the following letter to George from Santa Cruz, Trinidad in October 1956:

My dear George,

Of all the comments which have appeared in the Press and elsewhere in connection with my decision to stop playing first-class cricket I appreciated yours the most and I wanted you to know this in case you did not know it before. I have realised for some time now that ever since I was of an age to appreciate the finer points of our game I learned more of cricket strategy and tactics from you than from anyone else. Unfortunately I was never able to discipline my own cricket to the extent that I would have liked. If I could have done this I would probably have made many more than I did.

The boys told me in B G that you are getting along well and doing a fine job of work. Gilchrist and Dewdney appear to be our best prospect for pace in 1957.

Hope you do not mind me writing but I wanted to thank you for your help over the years.

Very sincerely yours,

Jeffrey.

Incidentally, it is interesting to note that both Learie Constantine and C L R James thought that the West Indies would not have lost the 1951-52 series in Australia if George had been manager and the tourists had been able to draw on his wisdom and experience, not to mention the effect his mere presence would have had on the side.

Meanwhile, difficulties with some of the members at Lucas prompted him to join Kensington Club next door in 1947, the same year they attracted Frank Worrell to their ranks. He played for Kensington until he went to England in 1950, and resumed his career with them five years later when he returned home as national cricket coach. At the end of that season he decided to retire from Senior Cup cricket to concentrate on his coaching commitments. His most memorable innings in that final season was in a hard-fought match against Garrison. All the panache of his youth returned as he lashed into the bowlers for 120. The innings was recalled in a souvenir programme issued by Kensington in 1970 as "indelible to spectators who saw it". The writer went on: "I have seen Headley improvise many marvellous strokes, yet few equalled the mathematical precision with which he wristily back-drove a fast rising inswinger from Calbert Minott to chime on the screen board, in that match against Garrison."

The wheel had come full circle. As a little boy George had watched his first Senior Cup match in Kensington Park from the vantage point of a guango tree just outside. He ended his Senior Cup career on that same ground.

CHAPTER ELEVEN
INDIAN SUMMER

I N late 1948 George sailed to England with the rest of the tour party for India, and boarded a plane from there to Bombay. Although many thousands of people from the subcontinent had emigrated to the Caribbean in the late 19th century, they had become imbued with many aspects of the West Indian way of life, and the people they were to meet during the cricket tour were from a very different culture.

The first Test was played in New Delhi, the new post-independence capital, although the splendour of the city was not matched by the tourists' accommodation which, fortunately, turned out to be the exception to the rule.

Early on in the tour George struggled and was disappointing in the first Test, where he made just two in a first innings total of 631 which meant he didn't have an opportunity to redeem himself later in the match. Soon after, the West Indies broke off from their tour of India to play some games in Pakistan. They took the train to Karachi and played a match against Sind. George did not take part in that fixture but played in a two-day game against the Commander-in-Chief's XI at the military base in Rawalpindi. In this match he had an opportunity to bowl and took six for 49 in the second innings to ease West Indies to a comprehensive victory.

The tourists then moved on to Lahore to play what was effectively an unofficial Test. The Pakistani openers put on a 100 for the first wicket before John Goddard tossed the ball to George; he soon had them in trouble and induced Imtiaz Ahmed to offer a catch to Stollmeyer, before the other opener, Nazar Mohammed, offered him a return catch off his own bowling. But his luck did not hold: attempting to make it a hat-trick of victims, George lunged forward to make another catch and fell and hurt his side.

The next day it was discovered that he had sustained a fracture; and so went into bat at number nine suitably strapped up. He played through the pain, mainly in partnership with Christiani, and finished the innings on 57 not out. The Pakistani batsmen did much better in the second innings without George to bowl at them and the match was drawn.

On reflection it would have been wiser for George to stay in Lahore to recover properly from his injuries but, instead, he was expected to travel around with the

team and was prescribed a succession of different treatments from a variety of doctors. As a result his health problems lingered and he was unable to take part in any of the other Tests.

West Indies won the toss in all five Tests and batted first on each occasion. In the first three matches they scored heavily in their first innings but lacked the firepower to bowl the stubborn Indians out twice. But it was a different story for the fourth Test in Madras when West Indies secured an innings victory, due mainly to a record opening partnership, supported by penetrative bowling. India went into the final match at Bombay determined to try and level the series. For the first time West Indies made under 300 runs, although the Indians batted poorly in their first innings so the tourists still had a substantial lead. In the end the home side were left chasing 361 to win in 395 minutes, with Vijay Hazare taking the attack to the West Indians by scoring at a run a minute. By the tea interval the Indians were within striking distance of their target and Goddard had to decide whether or not to take the new ball. The senior members of the West Indies side held different views on the matter and Goddard finally accepted George's argument, namely that the new ball should not be taken because the men who could used it most effectively, John Trim, Prior Jones and Gerry Gomez, were already tired and it would be harder for the batsmen to make runs off the old ball.

After tea Hazare was dismissed but Dattu Phadkar continued the assault. In the end honours were even as, in a nail-biting finish, India were left needing six runs for victory and the West Indies two wickets, but more importantly from a West Indian point of view, they had won the series one-nil.

Shortly before they headed for home, the tourists made a visit to Ceylon (now Sri

❏ Vijay Hazare, who liked to dominate the West Indian bowlers.

Lanka) off the south coast of India. Their hosts introduced them to the Ceylonese way of life: they visited Kandy, the ancient capital, admiring the impressive architecture and also visited other places of interest, where they enjoyed Ceylonese food and entertainment. Inevitably, they also played some cricket, including one match against Combined Colleges at Colombo Oval. George was invited to play if he felt fit enough. He had a net and decided to play but, with 30 to his name, twinges of pain returned and he was about to retire. However the opposing captain offered him a runner, which he accepted, and he went on to score exactly 100 before he was out, after sharing a fifth wicket partnership of 146 with Gomez.

The West Indies travelled from Ceylon back to Bombay and took part in a charity match before their journey home. When they reached London, Allan Rae left the tour party to return to his law studies, Jimmy Cameron boarded a ship for Canada and Everton Weekes travelled north to begin a career in league cricket with Bacup, thanks largely to George's contacts.

When the Jamaican maestro returned home, he had to face the responsibilities of a growing family which meant securing his financial future became more of a priority than his cricket.

By that time Ron was nearly 10 years old, and has vivid memories of his father's homecoming. George had brought the youngster a bat which laid in a large box in a room adjacent to the dining room, while the family enjoyed their first communal dinner for many months. Ron says: "I was so impatient to see the bat, I kept asking to get down from the table and eventually I was given permission. It was quite dark in the room where the bat was and I didn't realise that there was a stuffed tiger skin, complete with head looking upwards, in the same box as my bat. In my haste to get the bat, I ripped into the box and was suddenly confronted by this massive tiger head, eyes and teeth bared, looking up in semi-darkness. It terrified me and I ran screaming from the room. Dad thought this was hysterically funny, although he got into trouble with Mum!"

❑ *Lord Constantine and Sir Frank Worrell who, along with Headley himself, were at the forefront of the campaign for improvements in players' wages and conditions.*

CHAPTER TWELVE
A PROFESSIONAL CALLING

WHEN George returned from India in 1949 he resigned from the Labour Department and became an insurance agent for Manufacturers Life Insurance Company. This change in jobs affected his freedom to play cricket as previously he had only needed to obtain the necessary leave; now when he wasn't working, he was without a salary.

In December 1949 Jamaica held trials to decide on the final candidates to go to Trinidad for the trials for the tour to England in 1950. A member of the Jamaican Board contacted George and asked him if he would captain Jamaica in Trinidad. George said he would go, but not as captain; however despite his reply he received a letter appointing him skipper. George wrote to the Board declining the captaincy and also informed them that he would play as an amateur or as a professional as it suited him. In the case of the tour to Trinidad his terms were a fee of £120 if the Board wanted him to go. A few days later George met the President of the West Indies Board on Duke Street and the latter explained that they wanted him to go to Trinidad not to prove his capabilities, but to confirm his match fitness.

The matter remained in the air and a few days later Headley's letter to the Board appeared in a newspaper under the headline "Headley baulks at Captaincy, Not on Team". It explained that, with Headley's decision, the issue of the captaincy remained unresolved, while an accompanying article from Ivan Barrow expressed the wish that the matter should be quickly sorted out. Later Barrow wrote that "if through business reasons he [George] is unable to make the trip, there is nothing more to be said, but I refuse to believe that he would not accept the captaincy if able to go". Along with George's other followers, Barrow concluded that he hoped all obstacles in the way of George going to Trinidad would be removed.

The sports editor of the *Daily Gleaner* was not so sympathetic and attacked him in an article entitled "What Price, Headley?" He accused George of 'stalling' for his own purposes and hinted that he was doing so to capitalise out of the game. However, the editor did not have his facts right when he claimed the Board had made him a reasonable offer; at that stage they hadn't even replied to his letter, let alone addressed the question of a fee.

The Board were quite unrealistic to expect Headley to play without financial reimbursement: he now had a family to keep and insurance salespeople do not get paid when they are not working. But the matter could not be resolved and George did not go to Trinidad; Johnny Groves was named as captain of Jamaica for the trials instead. While the teams were in Trinidad, the West Indies Board made financial offers to Frank Worrell and Everton Weekes who were playing in the Lancashire League in England. Their clubs, Radcliffe and Bacup, therefore needed replacements and, aware of George's stand over selection, cabled offering him terms. In the end he accepted a contract with Bacup, on the same basis as Weekes had been there.

But it seems the West Indies Board were still hoping George would tour England in 1950 with the Test team. Before the tour party was announced, George was invited to attend a meeting with officials from the Jamaican Board. They showed him a cable indicating that because of the high costs involved in the tour they should find out whether George was willing to accept amateur status. George knew that Worrell and Weekes were being paid, so enquired about the fee for amateurs. He was informed that it would be £5 per week. He anticipated that this might have been the line of the discussion and produced the contract Bacup had sent him. The officials were surprised to learn that he had been offered the same terms as Weekes and George terminated the meeting by saying that he already had other commitments. He wished to earn his living as an established sportsman, not as an apprentice taking pocket-money. (Incidentally, Frank Worrell had made a similar stand, when he refused to tour India in 1948-49 after the Board failed to meet his pay demands.)

So, he returned to England in 1950 to play league cricket, although he did find time to attend the first Test at Old Trafford. Although Alf Valentine bowled well, the tourists lost the match, which prompted many of George's loyal supporters to call for his late inclusion in the tour party. But it would have been impractical at that stage, and the West Indies Board were not amenable to the idea anyway. Even so, after that early set-back West Indies fortunes took a dramatic upturn when they won the famous 'Calypso' Test at Lord's, and George was able to attend the Tests at Trent Bridge and the Oval, where they won again.

Before the season was over George negotiated another contract, this time with Dudley in the Birmingham League. He moved his family to Birmingham with him and settled down to play for Dudley before the call came for him to return to Jamaica in 1953. By that time many Jamaicans had settled in Birmingham and had kept a keen note of the considerable scores he was making for Dudley. They sent news of his success back to their families in Jamaica, which prompted a popular movement to bring him back home and therefore make him available for the series against England in 1954. As funds were needed to turn this dream into reality the *Daily Gleaner* opened a public subscription that collected over a thousand pounds.

George's friend, Harvey Depass, remembers how hesitant he was about returning to the Test match arena: "I told him he must go or he would be letting his people down. I am not sure why he was hesitant, maybe he felt his sight or reflexes were not up to it. He was a perfectionist and would have wanted to give 100 per cent. Having said that, I don't think the match would have been played if he wasn't in the side."

Headley arrived back at Palisadoes Airport in Kingston to a hero's welcome: cricketing enthusiasts young and old turned out to welcome him, those who had seen him play in his younger days and those who had only heard about his feats. He stayed briefly at South Camp Hotel, the scene of one of his first triumphal homecomings, but soon moved to private accommodation. His first invitation to play cricket came from the President of the Lucas. The club was arranging a fund-raising match and they knew if George took part it would bolster gate receipts. George, who was already a life member of Lucas, agreed. Unfortunately early in the match he sustained yet another injury, as this time the web between his third and little fingers was split as he took a catch.

During the time that his hand was healing, he was approached by H S Campbell, a member of the Jamaican Cricket Board and Manager of the Innswood Estates, who asked him to lead a team that would play against MCC on the Estate. As he knew most of the players Campbell mentioned, George agreed to the idea. But the English team under Len Hutton did not whip up the same enthusiasm among Jamaicans as Lord Tennyson's team had in the 1930's. Times had changed: there was a growing sense of nationalism and West Indians were keen to see their own people excel. Hutton didn't seem to appreciate this change of mood and appeared to resent the esteem in which George was held. Describing a scene in which George came out for net practice, he wrote "in a flash interest in the MCC players vanished".

In the match at Chedwin Park, Innswood, George had to face Fred Trueman before he had scored. A ball rose off a length and hit him on the left forearm which became numb; the

❏ *A more mature George appearing for a Commonwealth XI against an England XI at Kingston in Surrey in August, 1951.*

crowd booed their disapproval and a doctor ran onto the field to attend to George. Again Hutton was unimpressed with the attention the incident attracted. George resumed his innings and struck Trueman for six, and then hit four, before being dismissed.

George's injury deteriorated overnight so that by the next morning he could not raise his arm without considerable pain. He went to Kingston Public Hospital where the doctor told him he had a contusion of the radial nerve and that he should rest for 45 days. As a result, he missed the first match Jamaica played against MCC, but decided to risk it for the second. Despite being in considerable pain he scored 53 not out in support of J K Holt. His friend, Jack Anderson, wrote: "The Melbourne Park match (MCC against Jamaica) on the eve of the first Test, was drawn, due in the main to a fighting stand of 195 for the fifth wicket by Holt (152) and Headley (53), the latter almost one-handed due to an injured arm."

❏ *Len Hutton pictured in a more jovial mood than Headley found him on his return to Test cricket*

Then came the moment everyone had waited for: the announcement of the Test side. The selection committee consisted of 'Crab' Nethersole, captain, Jeff Stollmeyer, and vice-captain, Frank Worrell. However, Worrell was ill and not available for the match and Frank King, the fast bowler, was injured. In the event, they decided to pick a team that batted well down the order and George was included on that basis which meant, at the age of almost 45, he became the oldest man ever to play for West Indies in a Test match.

His selection was greeted with delight in Jamaica and prompted Jack Anderson, the cricket correspondent on the *Daily Gleaner* to write: "...his experience - particularly in the field - will alone be worth 50 to 100 runs"; although it must be said that not everyone shared this view and felt that, at his age, it was taking a big chance to play the injury-prone George.

A bright sunny day greeted the participants at Sabina Park. Stollmeyer won the toss and elected to bat. George went in at number six with the score on 286; the applause lasted from the time he appeared out of the pavilion until he reached the wicket. The mood was one of nostalgia and his supporters were willing him to succeed, just as they had done against Lord Tennyson, almost a generation ago. He placed the ball between two fielders to get off the mark, a seemingly innocuous move at the time, but it caused great controversy when parts of Len Hutton's book were subsequently published in Jamaica. He wrote that "knowing the possibility of more 'incidents' from this temperamental race of people whose partisanship might cause their enthusiasm to spill over at any moment, I decided to deal prudently with George." He elaborated on how he "instructed the England bowler to give Headley an easy ball to allow him to get off the mark and I asked the fielders to stand back so that he could do so."

It was a supremely insensitive and patronising remark that even the usually mild-mannered Headley could not let slip. He wrote the following letter to the *Gleaner* on 20 March 1956:

The Sports Editor, Sir

When one is selected to represent his country whether he is amateur or professional he automatically becomes an ambassador of goodwill even under the most trying circumstances. I wonder if Len Hutton as the first professional captain to lead an English team on tour had succeeded in doing so during the West Indies tour of 1953-54.

Having retired he decided to write his memoirs, including his experience of the West Indies tour. This he set about to do by magnifying the incidents, presumably to exonerate the conduct of his team on the field.

I am here concerned with the incident he referred to in Jamaica and involving myself in his article appearing in last Sunday's Gleaner.

When Hutton says that the trouble started with Trueman injuring Headley it is far from the truth. If there was any trouble....it was caused chiefly by the behaviour of his team which went a far way to incite the spectators, whose reaction was rather confined to verbosity than suggestion of physical violence. The one such "reported" incident - the Burke case - was overplayed (as they did other incidents) by the English writers who accompanied the team.

Hutton blamed my injury to a "not bumping" ball which I failed to hit because of my age, failing sight, timing and lack of opportunity to play first-class cricket over a period. I think later the same year towards the end of the English season I played against an England XI at Torquay for a Commonwealth XI and scored 66. Opposing me was the fastest bowler of the day - Frank Tyson. I also recall that the English press described the match as the "Taming of Tyson by Headley and Roy Marshall".

If Hutton had even extended me a single to get off in the last Test, to glory in it as he had done would have been in bad taste. But this, of course, was done to inflate his ego and support the then Reuter story that Hutton had generously "given" Headley a single. What he conveniently failed to state was his intended plan when I came in and what happened to it.

It happened that I came in when a wicket fell to the fifth ball of the over, and the clock showed that there was just enough time for the bowling of another over before lunch. Clyde Walcott, who had been batting for most of the morning was my partner. Any captain with common sense would have done what Hutton did, although not making it so obvious, by opening the field to allow the new batsman (myself) a single off the last ball so that I would have to face the next over right away. A badly needed wicket just before lunch would have been another feather to preen Hutton's astuteness.

As a player who could do a little thinking in such circumstances and who never shelters under or sacrifices his partner, rather in all humility I say I prefer to protect even to the cost of my wicket, I took up Hutton's challenge. I took "the generous" single and defeated his objective by not giving England the wicket they wanted, despite going to the end Hutton wanted me.

I wonder if the late Lord Hawke, who captained England and Yorkshire, was wrong when he said that a professional would captain England over his dead body - (as it seems is just what happened).

There might be some significance when we recall that Hutton was never selected captain of Yorkshire. It appears a bad way to go out of a great game that has done so much for all of us, by throwing acrimonious statements about.

I am etc.

Geo. Headley.

Returning to the match itself, George scored 16 in West Indies' total of 417 before he fell to Tony Lock. The best home batsmen were J K Holt who scored 94 and Walcott, who made 65. MCC replied with an impoverished 170 which left Stollmeyer in two minds about whether to declare. He sought the advice of George, who argued that despite the psychological advantage the West Indians would gain by enforcing the follow-on, their bowlers were too tired to take advantage of it. Stollmeyer followed George's advice, although the decision to bat again did not meet with the approval of all sections of the crowd. For a while it looked like their scepticism might be proved right: George only made one in West Indies' second innings total of 209 for six declared and the English, headed by Willie Watson, Peter May and Hutton, looked as though they might secure victory.

Stollmeyer had another conference with Headley who suggested that the bowlers should attack the leg-stump, backed up by a tight field. This restricted the English in their scoring and, in the end, Esmond Kentish in his one and only Test worked the oracle reaping five wickets for 49, as West Indies won by 140 runs. The critics were quickly silenced and Stollmeyer repeated these tactics in the Test at Bridgetown, which again brought West Indies a decisive victory.

CHAPTER THIRTEEN
DUDLEY DAYS

I N the summer of 1951 George joined Dudley cricket club, where he was to enjoy four seasons playing for them in the Birmingham League. He was signed to partner Bill Merritt who had just been reinstated as an amateur having served as a professional from 1946. Predictably George set a record in his first season by scoring 922 runs to beat the previous record aggregate of 878; and went on to score almost 3,000 runs in only four summers. As a bowler he reverted from his medium-pace to bowling spin, collecting 102 wickets (14.01) in all for Dudley. The nature of his contributions were revealed in a newspaper report of a match played against Aston Unity: "Dudley were in trouble until the eighth wicket at Hillcourt, after being put in by Aston Unity. Then professional, George Headley (95 not out) and spin bowler Tony Sherwood (44) came together to put on 80 to help put on a respectable total of 171." When it was Aston Unity's turn to bat, George bowled splendidly to return the figures of four for 32 off nine overs.

Despite having the services of George at their disposal during these years, as well as some gifted amateurs, Dudley only won the championship once, in 1952. Inevitably George played a major part in the success that year, scoring 169 not out in the rout of Mitchells and Butlers. Harry Thomas, with an unbeaten 62, helped to produce a match-winning score that day, as the pair put on 241 for the second wicket. (In a remarkable all-round performance, George then returned the bowling figures of 9-3-14-3.) Harry had fond memories of George: "The crowds came to see George. They really loved him; a benefit match in his honour once attracted 14,000 people. Many of the West Indian players appeared in that match, Weekes got 100 and George told them what to do against us!" Harvey Depass, a long-time friend of George's from Jamaica, remembers his generous nature which was revealed during that match: "The game attracted one of the biggest crowds ever, the ground was thronged with thousands of people. He had got together a star-studded line-up including Clyde Walcott, Sonny Ramadhin and Alf Valentine, Learie Constantine, J K Holt and Ken Rickards. At the end of the game, George asked the players what he owed them for their expenses. I remember Constantine's reaction, 'George wants to know how much he owes. Tell him to buy me a biro pen. He is mad, I will treasure that more than anything else.'"

Sometimes George's generous nature went too far, as Harry Thomas revealed: "In his first season at Dudley he stayed with Floss and Sid, who ran the local 'Swan Inn'. One night he organised a get together for the locals there and provided white rum that Rena, his wife, had sent from Jamaica. He called it 'Fire Water', which was a fairly accurate description. When Rena arrived in England, she was quite surprised to learn that George had administered it to us neat!"

The family had moved to Birmingham during his years at Dudley. Besides the change in temperature, they also had to get used to a change in diet. Being weaned on rice and peas, curried goat and patties, the family now joined the locals in dropping in for fish and chips. One of the things that made the transition for the Headleys so easy was the warmth of the welcome from the local people many of whom, like Harry and Sylvia Thomas, became firm friends.

Gordon Smith remembers George from his Dudley days too: "I was 15 in 1952 and remember a lot of his phrases. For example, he would always say two fours are better than a six. We were in awe of his ability, and he had so much time for the youngsters. It was always a great experience to bat with him. Even in friendly games he would give you sound advice and helpful little tips, and he helped me with my bowling. As a bowler himself, he took wickets because of his knowledge of the game rather than his ability; he could tell where a guy would play the ball by the position of his feet."

Smith himself had an unexpected opportunity to prove himself against high class opposition in 1952. "I was still at school at the time, but a West Indies XI were playing a Midlands XI in a charity match at Edgbaston and I got permission to take the day off to watch as the captain of Dudley, Tom Palmer, was my sports master. When I arrived Jack Flavell, who was in the Midlands team was injured, so I got the opportunity to play against the West Indies at the age of 15. West Indies won easily, but I got Clyde Walcott's wicket. Afterwards George came over to congratulate me on my famous scalp, which encouraged me to take the game more seriously. Today Smith is a successful businessman, but still a competent and serious cricketer.

In 1986 Dudley won the national village knockout competition, the William Younger Cup. The following year Smith was captain of Dudley and attended a reception given by Cockspur, the new sponsors of the competition. He says: "There were 11 England captains at the Cricketers' Club and I went as captain of the club that held the trophy. Sir Garfield Sobers was also there and, despite all the famous names he had played with, was extremely envious to learn that I had played cricket with the great George Headley!"

After George left Dudley at the end of the 1954 season they dropped to bottom of the championship in 1955, but recovered to take the title in 1957, by which time George's son, Ron, had joined their ranks. Indeed, he had made his second XI debut for Dudley in June 1952 and prompted the following newspaper comment: "Main point of interest in the Dudley innings was the first time appearance of Ron Headley, 14-year-old son of George Headley, Dudley's West Indian professional. The boy opened the innings and, in scoring 30 in 58 minutes batted extremely well before returning a catch to W Smith. His footwork and stroke-play were very good."

CHAPTER FOURTEEN
COACH AND MENTOR

I N 1955 George was invited back to Jamaica as national coach. Despite his success in England and, to an extent because of it, there was a desire by the Jamaican people to bring George home. This culminated in a public subscription which raised over £1,000 to pay for his passage back to the Caribbean to take part in the trials for the Test series against England in 1954. With the increased feeling of nationalism and looking towards independence there was a desire that leading members of the black community should take a more prominent role in public life. When he returned for that series George met Norman Washington Manley, who was then the leader of the Opposition in the House of Representatives, who told him they wanted to bring him home and involve him in the country's cricket programme.

The idea of appointing George as government coach was first discussed by Kingston City Council in 1954. The Ministry of Education and the Press became involved, while the Jamaican Cricket Board of Control was kept informed of developments. When the House of Representatives approved the appointment, the Cricket Board was invited to organise the coaching scheme. Initially, the Board declined the invitation but, before George arrived back from England, a formula had been worked out which was acceptable to the Board.

George returned home with his second son, Lyndie, while the rest of the family stayed in England. While they were at sea, elections were held in Jamaica and Norman Manley's People's National Party was voted into power, with the deputy leader being none other than 'Crab' Nethersole who had captained Jamaica at cricket and been a long-standing admirer of George's. It was the perfect political back-drop for him to begin his career as coach.

During his voyage, George worked out his coaching scheme which was to be all-embracing and which would involve him contacting all the schools and clubs on the island. He also wanted to find out about the exact relationship between himself and the Board and wrote them the following letter: "I find that by watching seasoned players in action they (the youngsters) can improve themselves equally well in all phases of the game and I respectfully recommend that whenever a visiting team is in the Island an arrangement be made with the Cricket Board of Control for the

❏ *Ron Headley, who played in two Tests for West Indies, recalls how his father feared 'overcoaching'.*

acquisition of, say, 50 tickets daily to be used on a roster basis daily throughout the tour to enable each of those selected to see at least one day's play. I would personally supervise their attendance throughout the day if the suggestion is approved."

With the election of the new government George's post came under the auspices of the Ministry of Social Welfare rather than Education and he worked from temporary offices at the Jamaica 300 Headquarters on Harbour Street. He had to submit his reports and itineraries to the Cricket Board and from the outset he was encouraged by Nethersole to make sure that events were not concentrated in Kingston and that rural areas benefited from the scheme as well.

He began his job by liaising with head teachers before going into schools for a week at a time. He visited high schools, approved schools, youth clubs, Boys' Brigade and Boys' Town. He began by giving them an introductory talk on the first afternoon and followed that up with a session on fielding practice. This approach was designed to quash the notion that only batting was important. On the remaining afternoons he devoted equal attention to batting, bowling and fielding with the regular games master in attendance, so he could remind his students of what George had said when they were left to their own devices.

Ron Headley remembers his father was ever fearful of overcoaching. The main attributes he looked for in a young player were natural ability and guts. He stressed the importance of guiding a youngster to make the most of his natural talents and did not believe it was possible to produce a cricketer from a textbook. Ron remembers a conversation that took place between George and a committee member at Dudley, while he was having a net with the senior players: "The committee man felt that I was holding the bat wrongly and wanted to know when Dad was going to correct me. He said he had no intention of altering my natural grip even if it was wrong according to the coaching manual. He argued that as long as I kept hitting the ball in the middle of the bat, then the grip must suit me."

Ron also remembers his father's concern at the amount of cricket that was being played in England as far back as the mid-1950's. He believed that young batsmen and, more especially, young fast bowlers would be 'burnt out' of the game before they had tasted Test cricket, and predicted the emergence of a pool of mediocre players as administrators sacrificed quality for quantity.

George's new coaching position in Jamaica meant that in addition to imparting technical knowledge about cricket to youngsters, he could also talk to them about life in general. He emphasised that to reach Test standard they would have to make a lot of sacrifices and also stressed the importance of maintaining their academic interests. Besides his coaching commitments George was frequently invited to present trophies and cups to winning cricket teams, and used those occasions to air his views on the best way to develop cricket on the island. He began this trend with his first presentation, when he awarded the Sunlight Cup to Kingston College who played at Clovelly Park where he had scored his first hundred. In his speech he argued that it would be better for schools to play six-ball overs rather than eight as had been introduced during the War years, saying it put too much physical strain on young people who were not yet mature athletes. He followed that speech up with a letter to the Board suggesting six-ball overs be introduced into Senior Cup and other domestic cricket under its auspices. The Board took his advice and it is perhaps no coincidence that several top class fast bowlers emerged during the period that George was coach.

He also suggested limited-overs cricket for colts, but the schools did not take up this suggestion. However, the Civil Service introduced it for the Hewson Shield as did the J K Holt Snr Memorial Cup competition, and later the Gillette Cup in England.

During his first year as coach, George made a comprehensive survey of the state of cricket on the island, noting promising cricketers and the facilities at their disposal including grounds and equipment. He kept in close contact with schools, both primary and secondary, urging teachers to pick out their promising players for the coaching sessions he organised as he travelled around the island. If the school had a playing field he would coach there otherwise he would arrange for them to be instructed on a communal ground. He coached schoolboys in the morning and adults in the afternoons and, as a result of his findings, urged the Cricket Board to call on each Parish Council to supply their parishes with a cricket ground for youngsters, and in the wetter parts to provide concrete pitches.

The rural areas, in particular, responded well to his enthusiasm and headmasters frequently organised transport to ensure that their youngsters reached a particular ground on time. And, like George in his younger days, lads who missed the trucks invariably walked five or so miles to take advantage of his coaching. George had such a following in the rural parts of Jamaica that on public holidays some of the locals would frequently organise a match against a team George would bring from Kingston. They were popular occasions and George always got a good side together that frequently included former Test players and members of the Board of Control.

The high schools in Greater Kingston took part in the Sunlight Cup competition, but the outer districts did not have such an incentive. Given the emphasis on including the rural areas this was looked on as a major omission and Eric Frater, then headmaster of Rusea's School in Lucea, decided to initiate a competition for these areas and got a trophy donated that he decided to name in honour of George. Before long the standards achieved in the George Headley Cup competition matched those of the Sunlight Cup.

When Australia visited the Caribbean in 1954-55, the St James Cricket Board asked George to captain an Invitation XI made up of promising youngsters against the tourists at Jarrett Park in Montego Bay. Unfortunately the weather ruined the match, and thus deprived the locals of some promising entertainment.

As part of young cricketers' education, George believed it was highly profitable for them to spend time watching some of the finest exponents of the game and had continually tried to persuade the Board to make tickets available to promising youngsters to watch games played by various touring teams. This, however, was deemed to be too expensive an exercise. But George acquired some tickets for the final Test against Australia in 1955 after a group of West Indians, who had been planning to come over for the match from America were unable to do so. They asked that their tickets be given to George to distribute to aspiring young cricketers. Although he only received them on the second day of the Test he went round the various schools to give the youngsters an opportunity to watch some top-class cricket.

By 1956, it was clear that George's workload was so heavy that he needed an assistant. So Dickie Fuller, the former West Indian all-rounder was appointed to help George in his task of co-ordinating a country-wide programme to improve cricketing standards throughout Jamaica. The Government were enthusiastic supporters of the scheme and built them offices and a practice ground at George VI Memorial Park, facilities they shared with Herb McKenley, who supervised track athletics on the island. In 1956 Headley and Fuller held coaching sessions at 422 schools and clubs, instructing over 2,000 schoolboys and over 900 club members and encouraged the circulation of the cricketing manual *Know the Game*.

That year was a special one for George as he was awarded the MBE in the Queen's Birthday honours list. The award was made by the Governor, Sir Hugh Foot, who read the citation amid

❏ *Dickie Fuller (right) with George Mudie at a reunion of former Jamaican Test players. Fuller was appointed to assist George with his coaching programme on the island.*

loud cheers: "He is recognised as the most brilliant cricketer ever produced by Jamaica. He is held in the highest esteem not only in Jamaica but also throughout the West Indies and in the whole world of cricket." Appropriately the ceremony took place at Sabina Park rather than Up-Park Camp parade ground, the usual venue.

Besides his commitments to school and estate cricket, George was also involved in the selection of representative teams to face touring sides and also in the preparations for when teams from Jamaica travelled overseas. He took part in the hectic preparations for the visit by the Duke of Norfolk's team in 1956 and also assisted the Monymusk Sugar Estate team that went to Trinidad to play the Caroni Estate team there.

In 1957 George resurrected the tour of the parishes by an All-Schools team chosen from players in the Sunlight Cup competition, that had originally been inspired by 'Crab' Nethersole. This tour took place during the summer holidays and was met with great enthusiasm by all the participants, and raised considerable interest on the island. Maurice Foster, who went on to play for the West Indies, was one of the batsmen to emerge from these tours but, after a few years, lack of funds meant they disappeared again.

Roy Gilchrist and Herbert Sewell were two of George's earliest discoveries. He first saw the pair in the Community Store Novel Knockout. Neither of them had played Senior Cup cricket, but he was impressed with them, particularly Gilchrist's ability to engender such pace, given his slight frame, and Sewell's control, that he invited them to his coaching sessions. George's favourable impressions about their ability meant they were soon elevated to Senior Cup cricket and took part in trials for Jamaica. It took Gilchrist about a year to make the Jamaican team and Sewell, too,

won that honour some time later. Indeed, Sewell achieved the rare distinction of bowling the great Pakistani batsman, Hanif Mohammed for a duck, at a time when he was enjoying great success in the Caribbean. Gilchrist went on to play Test cricket and, after his controversial departure from the international scene, played successfully in league cricket in England for many years. However, many promising youngsters never played representative cricket for Jamaica let alone the West Indies as they opted to pursue their studies in

❏ *Roy Gilchrist, one of George's earliest protégés, who blossomed briefly for West Indies before disagreements with the captain curtailed his career.*

America, while others signed contracts to play English league cricket. Clive Winter, for example, a former All-Schools captain went on to obtain a doctorate and a distinguished teaching career in the United States. Even so, others stayed to pursue a career in cricket and those coached by George and Dickie who appeared for Jamaica include A Chavis, W Warren, Lloyd Williams, C Headlam, F Harvey, S C Watson and Tom Dewdney. The last two also played for the West Indies, confirming the success of bringing on young fast bowlers during George's period as coach, it was also at this time that representatives from the rural areas first made the national side.

In 1958 further acknowledgements of George's contribution to the game came when he was made an honorary life member of MCC, an honour also bestowed on him by the Lucas Club he played for in the 1930's and the Kensington and Melbourne Clubs he appeared for in the 1950's. He was also a life member of the Queen's Park Cricket Club in Trinidad.

George also took teams from Jamaica overseas, invariably trying to get a blend of youth and experience. In 1958 he took a team to the Bahamas and in the one match he played in took four for 29! The following year he was invited to British Honduras (now Belize) to help their national side prepare for the first visit by MCC.

❑ *George pictured with the promising Collie Smith, whose career was cut tragically short by his premature death in a car accident.*

When Pakistan toured the Caribbean in 1958, he was able to revive his policy of taking up-and-coming cricketers to see first-class cricket. The Jamaican Board of Control approved of his idea to raise funds to buy tickets so schoolboys could attend the colony game and the Test match. In all he collected £68 which allowed 136 boys from different schools on the island to attend a day's play. Every day George and Dickie Fuller would wait for the youngsters at Sabina Park and would sit with them, pointing out various features of the day's play to help them develop their own game.

However, by the early 1960's, despite the magnitude of their achievements, Headley and Fuller came under criticism because were few Jamaican faces in the Test team. Gerry Alexander, Allan Rae, John Holt Jnr and Ken Rickards had retired in the 1950's and Collie Smith, who had such great potential, had been tragically killed. Indeed, Barbados was the dominant island contributing such giants as Worrell, Walcott, Weekes, Sobers, Hall and Griffith to the Test side. But those who attacked Headley's approach failed to grasp the nature of his task which was designed to raise the general standard of cricket on the island, while geniuses only emerge very occasionally; added to which it is a long process to go from promising schoolboy cricketer to established Test batsman, as Maurice Foster demonstrated. Fortunately the Government and Cricket Board appreciated the long-term nature of George's work and the less-informed finally quietened down. Indeed, the real value of his work came through in such contests as those between Jamaican and Barbadian schoolboys in Jamaica in the summer of 1961. The match that created the most interest was the one the tourists played against the Jamaican All-Schools. Reg Scarlett and Maurcie Foster, who went on to represent the West Indies, played in that match, as did Keith Boyce for Barbados, who also won Test honours.

Shortly after that series, George prepared for a six month coaching stint in Nigeria. The proposal had originally been put to him in 1955 when he first returned to Jamaica. During the voyage he met J R Bunting, ex-headmaster of Wolmer's Boys' School, who was then Director of Education in Nigeria. Bunting was returning for a holiday in Jamaica, but was keen to know whether George would be prepared to visit Africa to coach, as Nigeria had a number of talented cricketers. However, the discussions were only tentative, and George heard nothing more until Nigeria achieved independence in 1960. Encouraged by the change in the political climate, the Nigerian Cricket Association approached their government to try and obtain the services of George. The Nigerian government liaised with the Jamaican government and an agreement was reached whereby George would go on a six-month coaching contract.

He arrived in Western Nigeria at the end of September 1961 and was given a warm welcome by the Acting Premier and Minister of Economic Planning, C D Akran, and was informed that he was to be Nigeria's national cricket coach for the length of his stay.

He was soon into his job organising coaching sessions for the secondary schools and clubs in Lagos. As they knew very little about the rules of the game, George had to spend time going over these as well as the basics of batting, bowling and fielding. But his easy-going manner and sense of humour made the boys relax in his company.

Nigeria is much bigger than Jamaica and George often had to travel long distances to fulfil his obligations. But his pupils were always eager and having learnt both English and cricket at the various mission schools, there was no problem of communication. All they lacked was expert coaching and opportunities to practise and George intended to put that right.

Michael Arnold remembers when George visited the Ibadan Club in Western Nigeria: "The team at that time was predominantly British, with just one or two Africans in it. Towards the end of the practice period, after several willingly given and useful comments on our technique, George put on a pair of batting gloves, and armed only with a stump, asked us to bowl to him in the nets. He had no pads on - didn't need them - and for 10 or 15 minutes we bowled anything and everything we could at him. It was the most remarkable performance. He played every shot in the book, never looked at all uncomfortable, and his timing and execution was exquisite. The fact that he was holding a stump and not a bat was almost impossible to detect and the bowling, spin, medium and fast, was of a fairly high standard. He was then 53, and one could only surmise, in wonder, at what he must have been like in his prime."

The highlight of the cricketing year in Nigeria was the annual 'Test' match against Ghana. While he was staying in Nigeria one of these 'Tests' took place. It was an exciting contest: Nigeria led on the first innings with 158 runs to Ghana's 113 and after the visitors had made 139 in their second innings, Nigeria required just 94 for victory. In a tense finish they failed in their bid by two runs. During that match George was introduced to Nigeria's distinguished Governor-General, Dr Azikiwi, who had founded the independence movement in the country. After his departure, the Nigerian Cricket Association kept in regular contact with George and the following year he was delighted to learn that Nigeria had beaten Ghana by six wickets in Accra, the capital of Ghana, to take the Clerk-Omololu Cup.

❑ *George making a shot fit to grace any coaching manual.*

Before he left for home, George wrote a memorandum on the state of cricket in Nigeria with some suggestions for its improvement. He believed that the senior primary schools should be regarded as nurseries of cricket and suggested that clubs be formed within the schools to foster the game. He said they needed adequate facilities, including concrete cricket pitches, cricket manuals and an initial stock of equipment that they would have to replace themselves.

For adults, he suggested that an enclosed cricket field should be laid out in each region for inter-regional and international matches; also that the pitches should be of jute matting or Bitu turf, rather than the concrete and coarse matting which were then being used. He suggested too that a cricket board be appointed for each region and that sport, including cricket, should be regarded as an integral part of the country's education programme. He also hoped that a team of secondary schoolboys from the West Indies might be invited to tour Nigeria.

The Nigerians were delighted with what he had done for them and the Secretary of their National Cricket Association sent the following letter to the Ministry of Housing and Social Welfare:

Dear Sir,

I am directed by the Nigerian Cricket Association to inform you that Mr G A Headley successfully completed his six-month assignment as cricket coach in Nigeria, leaving here for home by air on Thursday, 29th March.

His stay was of immense value, and there is no doubt that the coaching scheme which he conducted was a huge success.

My Association is greatly indebted to your Ministry, and once again sends its thanks for affording it the opportunity of enjoying the services of such a renowned cricketer and coach.

Yours faithfully,

E O Oyesiku

In 1962 there was a change of government in Jamaica which seemed determined to shake up the various sports associations and encourage them to improve their coaching schemes. As a result of this the Cricket Board of Control held six special meetings and replied to the government that "two coaches could not satisfactorily coach all the persons available at all the centres throughout the Island in the time available each year" and recommended an increase in the number of coaches, given that Headley and Fuller had to cope with the expectations of 750 schools even before they could think of the needs of the clubs.

But the government ignored this advice, with the new Minister of Development and Welfare seemingly determined to impose more direct control over sports associations. This led to much wrangling and argument that, in some cases, went on for years. In his effort to enforce his will the Minister appointed a Director of Sports, who had no background in sport or its administration. Government coaches who had been treated as men who knew their jobs and as former sporting heroes in their own right found their schemes trapped in a web of bureaucracy.

It was commonplace that, in this new climate, George would map out a programme and hand it to the Director of Sports who would study it for several days, before adding a memorandum. The Director then sent it to the Secretary of the Social Development Commission who took his turn with it and then handed it to the Minister. The Minister would study it and it would then be sent back down the line, as coaches sat around awaiting instructions from men who knew nothing about the game anyway!

It was a thoroughly unsatisfactory situation and caused much heated debate in the Press. Meanwhile, George continued to do his best in trying circumstances and his services were greatly appreciated by those who benefited from them. However many of the schemes which now had government support were unworkable because they were more designed to reap political dividends than sporting ones.

Eventually the Minister found it impossible to control the sports associations despite controlling their finances, and decided that the government would no longer be responsible for coaching. As a result, most coaches were retired. Given George's public standing, the government were obliged to treat him honourably and the value of his pension was equivalent to his salary, as it was widely acknowledged that he had been underpaid in the initial stages of his contract.

❏ *That's George Headley!*

CHAPTER FIFTEEN
IS THAT GEORGE HEADLEY?

A FTER George retired he spent much of his time relaxing at home, especially on his verandah where it was cool and his friends could greet him as they passed by on the road. He remained a focal point for discussions on cricket and even youngsters, born after his international career was over, would seek him out for advice on some aspect of the game.

As an elder statesman of the game he was regularly invited to present prizes - including awarding the Senior Cup to the Melbourne Club in 1968, in the absence of the president of the Jamaican Cricket Association Cecil Marley, which set a precedent for George's services being requested on similarly important occasions - meeting various teams and attending special practice sessions. He was also involved in fund-raising activities and took part in functions to welcome overseas touring teams.

Besides awarding prizes, he collected a special one himself during a three-week youth cricket clinic held in 1970. After the session a Youth Award team was selected to play against some Jamaican Cricket Board XIs. George presented medals and certificates to those who had been selected for the youth team and encouraged the youngsters to "play cricket and see the world". Immediately after his speech, George was presented with a Jamaica tie by Vincent Hartley, the captain of the youth team, even though he had been retired from representative cricket for many years before Jamaica received Independence and had never been privileged to wear one. It became one of George's most treasured possessions.

Wherever he played cricket George was always the star attraction, although he invariably preferred to hide his identity, as his long-time friend, Errol Edwards, remembers: "He spent Christmas with me soon after the War, I think it was 1946, and we went out to the country to play a cricket match. Everyone knew his name, even if they did not know him personally. However, George was always shy and didn't want people to know who he was. On this occasion we were playing a friendly game in the parish of Hanover. I opened the innings with another chap who got out cheaply, and was then joined by George. It was a breezy day and the ground was elevated, which perhaps accounted for the fact that he seemed to be swaying as he walked to the wicket. One of the opposing bowlers commented, 'this one won't last long, he can hardly walk!' Three overs later he had over 50 runs to his credit, which prompted someone to remark that he batted like George Headley - even though he had never seen him. In the end rain caused the match to be abandoned; then someone realised that the batsman was George Headley and within a few seconds the crowd had surrounded our car.

"On another occasion we were travelling to another friendly match. Four of us, including George and myself, were in a car and the rest of the team and our supporters were in a lorry that had broken down. We got to our opponents' ground minus the rest of the team and said if they allowed us to bat first, the whole team could take the field later. I put on 30-odd with our opener, before he was dismissed. Then George came in and played his first ball for an easy run, but I did not run as I was busy admiring the stroke and, before I knew it, he was at my end and they had run him out for nought! I made some amends by putting on over 100 with the next chap. By the time it was our turn to field, our team still hadn't arrived, so we had to organise some substitutes until they showed up. But George was always an asset in the field, and if he missed out on the runs, he always wanted to make it up with his bowling. I seem to remember that he took quite a few wickets in that match and caused further excitement when a local policeman said it was George Headley bowling, but he kept on denying it. He opened the bowling for Lucas regularly in the War years and, although often successful, he would sometimes get hit about a bit. I remember on one such occasion his son, Ron, who was only about five at the time, shouted from the pavilion, 'take yourself off, Daddy!'"

Harvey Depass was someone else who knew George well in those days: "I got to know George in my teens when he played at Lucas during the War and I played for my college. In those days there were a lot of friendly games played around the country. We used to go to the sugar estates, enjoy a good day's cricket and eat curry goat. George taught me a lot about cricket. He would watch a youngster and knew immediately what he was doing wrong. I remember in one game we needed 20 runs to win and I went into bat at number seven. I hit the first ball I received into the covers and George came down the wicket to ask me what I was trying to do. I said, 'We've got to get the runs'; he replied, 'Just keep the castle intact and leave the rest to me!'

"One of George's great strengths was that he had eyes in the back of his head. The opposition would set a field to him, but he would always know if they moved a man finer. He also knew where he had placed a ball and would run without hesitation. He would always run the first run very quickly and then run three-quarters of the next and walk to finish it off. He had the skill to be able to do it at leisure. His eyes were always on the game whether or not he was batting himself. A chap would play a shot and you would hear him say 'two' as the batsmen set off. I don't think I ever met anyone who had such an instinctive understanding of the game as George."

That understanding, together with a long and distinguished batting career, brought George worldwide recognition. It also brought a great deal of memorabilia, although his early trophies had been lost in the cloudburst that swept away his home in 1933. He was certainly surprised to receive a call from a workman in 1974 to say that he had found a cup while doing some digging near George's former home. It turned out to be the cup presented by the Nestlé Milk Company, and a good polish revived the sterling silver, while a replacement base made it as good as new.

In his later years George remained involved with his former clubs, and often took part in activities at Lucas. On the occasion of their 75th anniversary he was invited to captain a Past West Indies players team in a fund-raising fixture against a Young Jamaican Team. George invited Berkeley Gaskin, the former Barbados and West Indian player, to be in his team, but he declined saying "George, you don't know your limitations. I know mine." However, Gaskin could not sap George's enthusiasm and he led out a side whose players included J K Holt Jnr, Alf Valentine, Allan Rae, Easton McMorris, Esmond Kentish, Jackie Hendriks and Gerry Alexander. The Young Jamaican team included Renford Pinnock (captain), Bruce Wellington, Arthur Barrett,

Linden Wright, Castel Folkes and Victor Fray. The match brought an enthusiastic response from the public, who packed the Nelson Oval, as the spirit of Senior Cup cricket in the 1940's was revived; indeed, many who were there that day had never seen George play.

The day before the match George had celebrated his 61st birthday and there was a great sense of anticipation as he walked to the wicket. He seemed to be timing the ball well but, in the event, only made three runs. He performed well in the field although Arthur McLean, a Lucas stalwart

❏ *George being greeted at the funeral of Lord Constantine.*

for many years, thought he was looking tired and offered him a pick-a-back ride into the pavilion which caused the crowd great amusement when he accepted. In the end, George was pleased to settle for a tie.

For several days after the game his muscles ached and he thought of Berkeley Gaskin's words. Perhaps from now on, he would stick to presenting the prizes! His resolve was tested when the following year Kensington invited him to lead a side of 'Old Timers' against the current players. It was a tempting offer and at first George accepted, but then wiser counsel prevailed and he enjoyed the match from the stands.

Beside his involvement in cricket, George's stature was such that he was invited to take part in many things away from the field of play. One of his sadder tasks was to attend the state funeral of Lord Learie Constantine in July 1971 as the representative of the Jamaican Board of Control. Before he left for Trinidad, he wrote the following obituary that appeared in the local paper:

During the month of November 1929 I was asked by a member of the Cricket Board of Control to be available for selection for the West Indies in the forthcoming tour of the MCC for the first Test match in Barbados. I accepted and proceeded there by ship. Learie and I were room-mates.

When the team was selected for the match I was included. Learie was the first person to congratulate me on my selection and I can still remember his voice and his comment, as he exhorted me: "George, play within your capabilities, it's just another match." That advice was an inspiration that stood me in good stead throughout my career.

As a cricketer, Learie was most dynamic in all departments of the game and there is no doubt that in his era he was considered the best all-rounder throughout the cricketing world.

I have travelled on many occasions with him and certainly did enjoy his company, especially because I found in him a man of great depth. No wonder down the years he made such a great impact not only on the cricketing world but as an international figure in the field of human relationships and otherwise.

I, for one, was not only proud but was not surprised that he attained such recognition, when he was created Lord Constantine.

To Lady Constantine and family I extend my heartfelt condolence.

May he rest in peace...

George and Learie held each other in the highest esteem, and shared many battles as they struggled for recognition for their people. Of George, Constantine had written: "I am fortunate to have seen West Indies rise from nothing to its pinnacle. I am fortunate to have been part of its achievements of 1950. So I saw every great Test innings played by Headley in England, Australia and the West Indies. But he [Headley] will never receive due recognition of his contribution to West Indies cricket, that is from the West Indies, because success in world affairs by a black man was not easily accepted by the powers that be. Somehow world recognition appeared to rid the area of domestic adulation with consequent local or West Indian's disinterest."

George received a warm welcome in Trinidad and was touched that he was still so revered in the Eastern Caribbean. The funeral, held in the Cathedral of the Immaculate Conception in Independence Square in Port-of-Spain, ensured the gathering of some of West Indies' most distinguished cricketers including Jeff Stollmeyer, Gerry Gomez, Derek Sealy, Prior Jones, Tyrell Johnson, Rupert Tang Choon and Clarence Skeete. Clifford Roach was also there and when George spotted him in his wheelchair, he abandoned his reserved seat and went and sat with him. George had heard from Jeff Stollmeyer some months earlier that Clifford had lost both legs because of his diabetic condition, and he had begun a correspondence. Constantine's funeral was an occasion for reminiscences as well as sadness and the pair recalled how that throughout several partnerships neither had run the other out. Roach now told him that he was going to England to have artificial legs fitted.

Later that year, George enjoyed a much happier occasion when a sculpture of his head was unveiled at the National Stadium in Kingston. It was over 40 years since the idea of such a monument had first been mooted. Mr C R Harrison, a sports goods dealer, had first suggested it after George's two centuries in the Georgetown Test of 1930. The idea was revived when a sculpture of the head of Sir Herbert MacDonald was installed at the Stadium in 1968. The sculptor, Alvin Marriott, contacted George and explained that the Machado Sports Foundation had commissioned him to do a similar sculpture of George. George was hesitant at first, saying that he could use the bust of him that had been made in 1947. Marriott explained that it would have to be especially made for installation at the National Stadium and George agreed to sit for this new work. After a number of sittings a wax facsimile of his head was sent to England to be cast in bronze and, on its return, the unveiling ceremony fittingly took place at Sabina Park in February 1969.

Lady Bustamante, the wife of Jamaica's first Prime Minister, was invited to unveil the sculpture but was unable to attend. Even so, she sent the following message that George kept among his souvenirs: "I deeply regret that I am unable to attend this function, but it is with profound pleasure that I send this message on behalf of one whose worthy contribution to cricket will go down in the annals of history, classifying him as one of the 'greats'." However, it was two years before the head was mounted at the National Stadium and that was only prompted by a sports reporter from the *Gleaner* whose enquiries into its whereabouts jolted the Jamaica Cricket Association into action. It was decided the ceremony should take place during the Benson & Hedges Youth Tournament, to give young cricketers throughout the Caribbean a chance to enjoy the occasion.

It was a memorable ceremony attended by many leading cricketing figures, including Clyde Walcott representing Barbados, Joe Solomon for Guyana and Len Harkin of Trinidad & Tobago. Others included Ivan Barrow, who recalled how he had partnered George when he reached his second century of the 1939 Lord's Test, and went on to describe how George had overcome the ploys used by the Australians to limit his scoring in 1930-31. In Barrow's opinion Headley had no peer as a batsman in all types of conditions and concluded that George had almost single-handedly put West Indian cricket on the world map.

Allan Rae spoke on behalf of the Jamaica Cricket Association and described George as the first outstanding batsman produced by the West Indies, on a par with Victor Trumper, Jack Hobbs and Don Bradman. He had played for Jamaica for 27 years and maintained a consistently high standard.

Finally the moment for the unveiling arrived and George joined the Minister of Youth and Community Development, the Honourable Allan Douglas on the platform. The Jamaican flag was removed from the sculpture and the Minister congratulated George. George thanked him and during his speech noticed Clarence Passailaigue in the audience, who had travelled over 120 miles from Montego Bay to be present at the ceremony. He immediately recalled the world record partnership of 487 he had set with the 'Broom' in 1932 and invited Clarence on to the stage to receive the applause from the audience. It was a touching moment for the two men, who were by then both

❏ *Enjoying a benefit for Gary Sobers at the Desnoes & Geddes Double Wicket International Cricket Tournament at Sabina Park in 1972. From left: George Headley, Prime Minister Errol Barrow, Gary Sobers and Prime Minister Michael Manley.*

in their sixties. After the official ceremony was over, the personal congratulations continued well into the evening as George and 'Pass' mingled among the crowd. Everyone was delighted that he had invited Passailaigue onto the stage commenting that many of the youth gathered that day had never heard of his esteemed batting partner.

George's words and gestures on and off the field have provided many of his contemporaries with inspiration. Throughout his life he took a keen interest in the financial well-being of his fellow cricketers, and was an enthusiastic supporter of sponsorship for players and also benefit matches. He was quick to congratulate Desnoes & Geddes for sponsoring an International Double Wicket Competition for Garfield Sobers' benefit; and in the accompanying programme, Headley wrote: "During the years in which I played league cricket in England I observed that it was the practice to organise benefit matches for players who had given considerable service to the great game called cricket. It was my privilege to participate in such matches. I noticed that while contributing to one individual financially these benefits also acted as an inspiration to other cricketers and to many youngsters to excel at the game. To this end let me congratulate Desnoes & Geddes for introducing the idea to Jamaica. It is fitting that you should start with our West Indies captain, Gary Sobers, who is universally regarded as the world's greatest all-rounder in cricket. It is my hope that your firm will consider this as only the first of such ventures and will endeavour to hold other benefits for cricketers who are now serving the game well."

In October 1973 George was given an even more prestigious honour when he received the Award for Excellence in Sports from the Norman Manley Foundation. The award is an annual presentation made to someone who shows excellence in their chosen field; the identity of the recipient is usually kept secret and it was only the week before the ceremony that George learned he was to receive the award.

The ceremony was held at the National Stadium, and 35,000 spectators crowded in for the event. Among the distinguished guests, apart from George himself, were the Governor-General the Most Honourable Florizel Glasspole, and Prime Minister Michael Manley. A hush fell over the crowd as they waited to hear who had been chosen for the award, and their anticipation was heightened as Douglas Graham explained the nature of the award. When George Alphonso Headley's name was read out there was a huge roar of approval from the spectators.

George stepped forward, wearing his West Indies tie, to hear the citation read by Douglas Fletcher, Jamaica's ambassador to the United States:

It is fitting that the field of Sports should be singled out for the Norman Manley Award of Excellence. Fitting because the late Norman Washington Manley was, among other things, a celebrated sportsman winning more events in Inter-Schools Athletics Championships than anyone else has ever done, and setting a record for the 100 yards which stood unbeaten for nearly half a century. Without any loss of interest in the field of Sports, he was to move on in adult life to a legendary professional career and a political life of creative dimensions to which the present generation owes not a little.

It is significant that his rise to prominence in public life in Jamaica should have coincided with the greatest deeds of the winner of the Norman Manley Award for Excellence in 1973 - George Alphonso Headley. George Headley can be described as humanist, coach of cricket, star of cricket, one of the greatest sportsmen of the twentieth century. George Headley is undoubtedly one of the greatest cricketers who ever lived, the best ever produced by Jamaica, the best batsman ever to appear in West Indian cricket and certainly among the few batsmen of excellence ever produced by the seven major cricketing countries since organised competition of this international game began.

This is, indeed, an achievement of distinguished eminence, by any standard, and the achievement stands as a model for Jamaicans today, as it will for generations of Jamaicans to come, in the struggle to build a society on the basis of sustained industry and application and commitment to excellence. For George Headley had a remarkable length of service in a Test career which began in 1930 and ended in 1954, a time-span exceeded only by two other players among the thousands who have played Test cricket over the past 96 years. He also scored double centuries for Jamaica more than 20 years apart, in noble defiance of a World War that threatened in 1939 to tarnish the glories of a career which he had nurtured throughout the decade.

He began his Test career by scoring over a century and three-quarters in the second innings of his first match which took place in Bridgetown, Barbados which, as it happened, was the hometown of his Barbadian father. In his own person George Headley represented some fascinating aspects of West Indian history and social life.

He was born in the Canal Zone of Panama, the son of parents who were among those who built the Canal with their labour. Fortunately, the matriarchal tradition prevailed and he was brought to his mother's homeland at an early age. Equally fortunate for Jamaica as for the West Indies, his cricketing talent saved him from joining relatives in the United States as a migrant himself. Instead, he stayed to become a cricket immortal at a time when opportunities were few, if not non-existent for persons born of George Headley's social background and circumstances.

It is this victory over severe odds through his dedicated artistry and brilliance that helps to mark George Headley, not only as a great sportsman, but a great human being worthy of emulation both in the world of sports and beyond.

His great scoring averages, his indomitable spirit on the field and his remarkable endurance all added up to style which helped to revolutionise the game of cricket, and has made his achievement to be of really original and lasting value.

To have scored the same number of centuries as matches played in his very first Test series; to have been voted the best leg-side player in the world by conquering a known weakness in the leg or on-side area of his batting; to have set up a world record for first-class cricket in the now famous Headley-Passailaigue partnership of 1932; to have remained, after a generation, still among the very few choice players of substance and exceptional brilliance - all serve to indicate the measure of the greatness of George Alphonso Headley.

As far back as 1933 his skills received the critical acclaim reserved for only the greatest. According to E W Swanton, the famous authority on cricket, in the second volume of the standard History of Cricket, *he had all the outstanding qualities of a*

❏ *George receives an award from the Governor-General of Jamaica.*

'superb wrist and eye of the finest...athletes and, what is less common, a calm temper...capable of stemming misfortune'. The tribute paid to him in his historic achievement of being 'the one and only man to score two hundred runs in a Test at Lord's' the home of cricket - remains true almost 35 years later! The interruption of World War II failed to break his spirit or his skill and, with peace restored, he was to engage in numerous inter-territorial games for Jamaica. Then, in a belated token gesture of justice, he was asked to captain the West Indies in one Test, and toured India in 1948-49, playing in a Test series in what was his 40th year. His magnanimity and love for the game as well as his quiet dignity made him carry on.

In 1954, at the age of 45, he was still good enough to earn a place in a Test side playing alongside new stars like Ramadhin and Valentine who were young enough to be his sons. Two of George Headley's sons were later to excel in cricket and athletics, due no doubt to the example and inspiration of their father.

For George Headley continues to be a living inspiration to the young. His presence in any company is the presence of sustained work, dedicated application and depth of concentration, of the spirit of excellence, and the embodiment of the human will to triumph over threatening odds.

He remains one of the few Jamaicans of his generation with a genuine international reputation and survives with the love, affection and admiration of the broad mass of Jamaican people.

The 1973 Award for Excellence in the field of Sports goes then to this great Jamaican, George Alphonso Headley, a unique and great contributor to a great and unique game of international sport.

October 6, 1973

The framed award was then presented to George by Norman Manley's widow, Edna. It was one of the most moving occasions of his life, and he took a while to compose himself before replying to the expectant audience: "I am very honoured tonight, at having been awarded such a coveted and prestigious award as the Norman Washington Manley Award for Excellence, by Mrs Edna Manley, commemorating his memory.

"Not only am I honoured, but I am very proud that our National Game has been so recognised in the field of Sports and I must confess that I am greatly indebted to the late Mr N N Nethersole, popularly known as 'Crab', for the inspiration and assistance he gave me in my youth and I must also make mention of Sir Alexander and Lady Bustamante, also our National Hero, the late Norman Washington Manley.

"To the youths of my beloved country, Jamaica, who are engaged in any form of Sport, I would say that to become a good performer in any game of your choice, physical fitness creates an alert mind which will enable you to discipline yourself in all endeavours. I would also advise you to have respect for authority.

"And now my innings has come to an end, being bowled by no other person than the Right Excellent Norman Washington Manley."

As if all this excitement were not enough, eight days later on 14 October 1973

George received the Order of Distinction. The occasion featured a military parade, followed by a religious service supported by a 150 voice choir and massed bands. Then came the national awards and honours for distinguished service to the nation that covered such diverse fields as anthropology, medicine, education, sports, journalism and national defence. It was a telling sign of his standing in Jamaican society that the applause lingered the longest when his name was called. The next day, National Heroes Day, a cricket match was played between Kensington's 'Old Timers' and an Under-23 XI to help raise funds for a nursery being built to accommodate promising youngsters. George was asked to plant a tree behind the southern boundary to commemorate his first view of a formal cricket match when, at the age of 11, he and his cousin enjoyed a grandstand view of the match by climbing a tree just outside the Kensington Club. Unfortunately a heavy cold prevented him from obliging them, but it was appropriate that the task was performed by Harold Noad, Kensington's oldest member, who had been associated with the club for over 60 years.

CHAPTER SIXTEEN
CLOSE OF PLAY

REDICTABLY, it was C L R James who summed up George Headley's batting genius when he wrote in *Beyond a Boundary*, "With him batting was first, not second, nature" and, further, "contrary to all belief, popular and learned, Constantine the magician is the product of tradition and training. It is George the maestro who is an absolutely outstanding cricketer."

Headley has assured his place in cricketing history as one of the finest cricketers ever to come out of the Caribbean; indeed, he is widely acknowledged as one of the greatest batsmen ever, and the dispute over the relative merits of George Headley and Sir Donald Bradman will doubtless continue for as long as cricket is played.

Statistics tell us a lot, but not the whole story. George scored 2,190 runs in 22 Tests at an average of 60.83; Bradman scored 6,996 runs from 52 Tests at an average of 99.94. Headley scored a Test century every fourth innings, whereas Bradman scored a century every two-and-a-half innings. On this analysis, Bradman seems to have a clear edge over Headley. However these statistics do not reveal that, at his peak in the 1930's, the Jamaican scored a century ever other Test, while the remaining West Indian batsmen could only manage five hundreds between them. The most incredible fact about Headley's batting was that, probably uniquely in the history of the game, he invariably had to stand alone against phenomenally powerful English and Australian sides: in 15 out of 35 West Indian Test innings he top-scored, in 11 of those he made at least a third of the runs and in three his contribution was over half the total score.

C L R James says: "This is what he carried on his shoulders for nearly 10 years. None, not a single one of the great batsmen, has ever been so burdened for so long." By contrast, Bradman could look to the likes of Bill Ponsford, Bill Woodfull, Jack Fingleton and Stan McCabe for support who, between them, had 27 Test centuries to their credit.

Pride of place in James' list goes to Bradman but he is quick to add "...it is my belief that if he had lived his cricketing life in England or Australia he would not be behind anyone." Even taking into account Headley's marked superiority over Bradman on difficult wickets, James still puts the Australian top of the pile, justifying his argument thus: "It is easy to give figures and make comparisons and draw rational

conclusions. The fact remains that the odds were 10 to one that in any Test Bradman would make 150 or 200 runs, and the more the runs were needed the more certain he was to make them. Yet if Bradman never failed in a Test series, neither did George. I believe Bradman and Headley are the only two between the wars of whom that can be said. (Hammond failed terribly in 1930 in England and almost as badly in the West Indies in 1934-35.)"

The celebrated commentator, Sir Neville Cardus believed that Headley had some claims to be considered a better batsman than Bradman on all types of wickets. In 15 innings on bad or wet wickets played between 1928 and 1938 Bradman averaged just over 16 runs, and passed 50 only once, 40 only twice and 15 only four times; while in 13 innings played in similar conditions during West Indies' tours of England in 1933 and 1939, George averaged almost 40. The Jamaican once remarked: "On a bad wicket it was you and the bowler. If he pitched up you had to drive. If he pitched short you had to turn and hook. No nonsense."

For myself, I am inclined to share Cardus' view. The fact that he went to the wicket aware that it was more rather than less likely that he would find little support from his colleagues must have put him under tremendous pressure. His talent was such that, despite this handicap, he was able to set new standards of

❑ *Donald Bradman, pictured in 1948, and the subject of so many comparisons - more or less favourable - with Headley.*

batsmanship. He carried the pre-war West Indian batting, like Manny Martindale did the bowling, but even his genius could not always bridge the gap (and George was the first to acknowledge, and remind others, that he could only bat so long as there was someone with him at the other end) as reckless strokeplay from others squandered any advantage the bowlers might have gained. Even so, in Tests he scored 10 centuries, converting two of them into double hundreds. Still one of the most impressive aspects about Headley's batting was that support was rarely forthcoming from his colleagues and he invariably had to stand alone. Harvey Depass argues: "Bradman could afford to take chances, George never had that liberty as he was the spine of the West Indian batting."

Perhaps the most fitting epitaph on Headley's career came from Berkeley Gaskin, who played under him in the Bridgetown Test of 1948. When asked, several years later, how he would compare the Jamaican with the then outstanding players, headed by the three 'W's and Gary Sobers, he replied: "They could sit in the same cathedral as George, but not in the same pew."

One of Headley's most recent accolades came at the end of 1988 when he was voted West Indies' all-time number three batsman and captain - ahead even of Frank Worrell - in a competition to decide the best-ever West Indies XI run by *The Cricketer* magazine, whose panel of judges included Viv Richards and Colin Cowdrey.

Indeed, his achievements on the field of play are beyond reproach but, in many respects, it is the socio-political environment in which he achieved them that magnify their importance. It can be argued that his outstanding sporting career coincided with and, in some ways, speeded social progress for blacks, (as when he went from sharing a bed with Learie Constantine in his early Test days to rooming with Jackie Grant, the white, amateur captain later in his career). To sum up, Headley was so gifted it was impossible for the selectors to ignore him and by his mere presence in the Test team he challenged the social mores of the time. Even so it was an uphill struggle: a white West Indian captain George played under once remarked, "We play cricket together and we worship together, but socially we do not mix"; and as late as 1948 the captain of the Barbados team held a cocktail party for the touring MCC side with only white or near-white members of the host side being invited. Indeed, George, who was captain of the West Indies team at the time, did not hear about the gathering until the next day.

Generally, there were tremendous social and political pressures on him as a young man who fraternised with the elite of Jamaica's colonial society by virtue of his cricketing gifts. He believed that a black man had to be 30 per cent better than a white man to get the same rewards and, in his early years at least, he was essentially a conformist. One of his sayings was "when in Rome do as the Romans do": he knew he couldn't change the situation on his own even if he wanted to (he was, incidentally, a great royalist and treasured his MBE although, unlike Learie Constantine, he was never knighted) and preferred to score political points with his bat.

Headley's social life was a rich mixture of cricket, working as a civil servant, daily Bible readings, relaxing with friends away from the public glare, various liaisons with different women - which included two marriages and nine children - and gambling, indeed a colleague from Dudley recalled how George would "bet on anything, even two flies climbing up a wall!"

Above all, however, he was concerned for his fellow human beings. He fought for improved wages for his team mates and, although he had a comfortable lifestyle, his concern was always for his peers who were less well off than himself, and he had several wrangles with the West Indies Board on this matter. His own cricketing gifts had brought their own, often material, rewards. His family were comfortably off - they had two maids - but, all his life, George remained a man of the people. He was happiest in the company of fellow cricketers and friends in Jamaica where, briefly, he could relax away from public view. His friend, Harvey Depass, remembers him as a down-to-earth character: "He never looked down on anyone. At Sabina Park you would never find George sitting in the pavilion, he would always sit with other spectators. He was revered by the people and even in the rougher parts of the island, you were safe if you were with George. I remember a story about a guy who broke into his house with the intention of stealing from it, but as soon as he saw some of the mementoes and realised it was George's house, he left without touching a thing!"

Although George could never be described as aloof, his celebrity status occasionally put him in a dilemma and this is aptly illustrated by his attitude to cars: he refused to learn to drive (very few black people

❏ *Berkeley Gaskin, who didn't believe even the most gifted of modern West Indian players ranked with the great George Headley.*

owned motor cars in those days) yet he didn't mind being driven round by his chauffeur. However, they always had to drive slowly so that George could acknowledge the locals who called out to him from the bars and shops as they travelled around Kingston. His inability to drive often proved a handicap to Depass: "When he was at Dudley we used to go into town on my motor bike. He would sit on the back wearing his trilby; the journey should have taken us about 10 minutes, but if George was a passenger it was nearer to half an hour because he always had something to say which meant I had to keep stopping the bike to hear what he was talking about!"

As a cricketer, and more especially as a Test player, George regarded himself as an ambassador for his country. Constantly under scrutiny because of his ability and his colour, he guarded his public image vigorously. He knew there were some people always waiting for him to make a mistake, but his conduct was impeccable and he never aired his grievances in public. For example, he was bitterly disappointed at being passed over for the West Indies captaincy initially, but expressed those feelings only to his family and intimates. His disappointment didn't stem from any egotistical desire, but rather from his belief that it was important for

❏ *Dean Headley, who has inherited an awesome cricketing pedigree.*

West Indian cricket that his knowledge of the game and players should be utilised to the fullest extent.

Two of George's children achieved international distinction in sport, Ron in cricket and Lyndie in athletics. Ron, an attractive left-handed batsman, played in the north of England leagues and for Worcestershire for many years with considerable success; indeed, his fine batting and brilliant close fielding helped Worcestershire to their first county championship in 1964. He also appeared for Jamaica and Derbyshire and won brief recognition at Test level in 1973, when he played in two Tests against England. Ron's son, Dean, continued the family link with first-class cricket when he signed briefly for Worcestershire in 1989, and has since appeared for Middlesex and, more recently, Kent. Lyndie was a member of Jamaica's sprint relay teams which won gold and silver medals in the Central American and Caribbean Games and Commonwealth Games of 1966. Two years before, at the Olympic Games in Tokyo, he reached the semi-final stage of the 100 metres and was a member of the team which came fourth in the final of the 4 x 100 metres relay.

However, despite these worthy achievements both men lived in the shadow of their famous father, who is remembered both for his remarkable sporting record and, perhaps more importantly, the difficult circumstances in which he became a cricketing legend. When George died in 1983, his followers knew not only had they lost a great sportsman but, in addition, a man with high humanitarian credentials who cared passionately for the welfare of his fellow human beings.

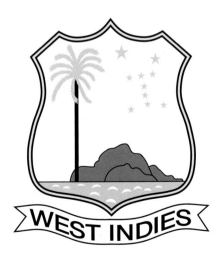

George Alphonso Headley

Date of Birth: 30th May 1909, Panama, U.S.A.
Died: 30th November 1983, Kingston Jamaica
First class debut: 9th February 1928 Jamaica v L.H. Tennyson's XI
Test match debut: 11th January 1930 West Indies v England
Teams: Jamaica, West Indies, Combined Jam/BG XI, Commonwealth XI, L. Parkinson's XI

Triple centuries (1)

Season	Runs	Venue	Team	Opponents
1931-32	344*	Melbourne Park	Jamaica	L.H. Tennyson's XI

Double centuries (8)

Season	Runs	Venue	Team	Opponents
1927-28	211	Melbourne Park	Jamaica	L.H. Tennyson's XI
1929-30	223	Sabina Park	West Indies	England
1933	224*	Taunton	West Indies	Somerset
1933	200	Derby	West Indies	Derbyshire
1934-35	270*	Sabina Park	West Indies	England
1939	227	Lord's	West Indies	Middlesex
1939	234*	Trent Bridge	West Indies	Nottinghamshire
1946-47	203*	Sabina Park	Jamaica	Barbados

Centuries (24)

Season	Runs	Venue	Team	Opponents
1928-29	143	Sabina Park	West Indies XI	Julien Cahn's XI
1929-30	176	The Oval	West Indies	England
1929-30	114	Bourda	West Indies	England
1929-30	112	Bourda	West Indies	England
1930-31	131	Melbourne	West Indies	Victoria
1930-31	102*	Brisbane	West Indies	Australia
1930-31	113	Melbourne	West Indies	Victoria
1930-31	105	Sydney	West Indies	Australia
1931-32	155*	Sabina Park	Jamaica	L.H. Tennyson's XI
1931-32	140	Sabina Park	Jamaica	L.H. Tennyson's XI
1933	129	Lord's	West Indies	M.C.C.
1933	129	Cardiff	West Indies	Glamorgan
1933	169*	Old Trafford	West Indies	England
1933	182	Edgbaston	West Indies	Warwickshire
1933	167	Folkestone	West Indies	England XI
1934-35	127	Melbourne Park	Jamaica	M.C.C.
1935	134	Blackpool	Lindsey Parkinson XI	Leicestershire
1935-36	118	Sabina Park	Jamaica	Yorkshire(Tourists)
1938-39	160	Queen's Park Oval	Jamaica	Trinidad
1938-39	103	Queen's Park Oval	Jamaica	West Indies XI
1939	103	Cambridge	West Indies	Cambridge University
1939	116*	Chelmsford	West Indies	Essex
1939	106	Lord's	West Indies	England
1939	107	Lord's	West Indies	England

Three centuries in successive innings

106 & 107 v England at Lord's, 234* v Nottinghamshire at Nottingham, 1939.

Career Record

Season/Team Opponents	V	BATTING									BOWLING				
		M	I	No	Runs	H.S.	Avge	100	50	CT	OV	MD	Runs	W	Avge
1927-28 Jamaica															
L.H. Tennyson's Tourists	WI	3	5		409	211	81.80	1	2	2	7	2	17	1	17.00
1928-29 Jamaica															
Julien Cahn's Tourists	WI	2	4		139	57	34.75		1	6	21	3	73	1	73.00
1928-29 West Indies XI															
Julien Cahn's Tourists	WI	1	2		187	143	93.50	1							
1929-30 Jamaica															
M.C.C. Tourists	WI	2	3		188	72	62.66		3	5	10	1	31	0	
1929-30 West Indies															
ENGLAND TESTS	**WI**	**4**	**8**		**703**	**223**	**87.87**	**4**		**4**	**23**	**2**	**77**	**0**	
1930-31 West Indies															
Tour of Australia	A	8	15		730	131	48.66	2	4	6	7	0	39	0	
AUSTRALIA TESTS	**A**	**5**	**10**	**1**	**336**	**105**	**37.33**	**2**		**1**					
1931-32 Jamaica															
L.H. Tennyson's Tourists	WI	3	4	2	723	344*	361.50	3	1	2	11	1	39	1	39.00
1932-33 Combined J/BG XI															
Combined Trin/Bar XI	IIs	1	2		51	30	25.50								
1933 West Indies															
Tour of England	E	20	32	2	2043	224*	68.10	6	10	13	211.2	35	640	21	30.47
ENGLAND TESTS	**E**	**3**	**6**	**1**	**277**	**169***	**55.40**	**1**	**1**	**4**	**19**	**1**	**81**	**0**	
1934-35 Jamaica															
M.C.C. Tourists	WI	2	3		152	127	50.66	1		1	3	0	20	0	
1934-35 West Indies															
ENGLAND TESTS	**WI**	**4**	**6**	**1**	**485**	**270***	**97.00**	**1**	**2**	**4**	**5**	**3**	**3**	**0**	
1935 L Parkinson's XI															
Leicestershire	E	1	2		152	134	76.00	1			8	0	37	1	37.00
1935-36 Jamaica															
Yorkshire Touring XI	WI	3	5		266	118	53.20	1	2	3	44	9	91	1	91.00
1938-39 Jamaica															
Trinidad	IIs	1	1		160	160	160.00	1		3					
West Indies XI	WI	1	1		103	103	103.00	1							
1939 West Indies															
Tour of England	E	17	25	6	1411	234*	74.26	4	6	10	6	1	13	1	13.00
ENGLAND TESTS	**E**	**3**	**5**		**334**	**107**	**66.80**	**2**	**2**		**4**	**0**	**17**	**0**	

Season/Team Opponents	V	BATTING									BOWLING				
		M	I	No	Runs	H.S.	Avge	100	50	CT	OV	MD	Runs	W	Avge
1945-46 Jamaica															
Trinidad	IIs	3	4	1	170	99	56.66		2	3	43	8	137	8	17.12
1946-47 Jamaica															
Barbados	IIs	2	3	3	339	203*		1	2	2	43	12	102	5	20.40
1947-48 Jamaica															
British Guiana	IIs	2	2	1	40	36	40.00			2	75	10	227	5	45.40
M.C.C. Tourists	WI	2	2	1	101	65	101.00		1	1					
1947-48 West Indies															
ENGLAND TESTS	WI	1	2	1	36	29	36.00				6	1	11	0	
1948-49 West Indies															
Tour of India	I	2	2		9	8	4.50			1	48	4	95	3	31.66
INDIA TESTS	I	1	1		2	2	2.00			3	0	18	0		
Tour of Pakistan	P	1	1	1	57	57*			1	1	20	11	21	2	10.50
1951 Comm. XI															
England XI	E	1	1		20	20	20.00		1						
1952 Comm. XI															
England XI	E	1	2		159	98	79.50		2						
1953-54 Jamaica															
M.C.C. Tourists	WI	1	2	1	58	53*	58.00		1		13.3	3	30	1	30.00
1953-54 West Indies															
ENGLAND TESTS	WI	1	2		17	16	8.50			1	5	0	23	0	
1954 Comm. XI															
England XI	E	1	1		64	64	64.00		1						
Jamaica		27	39	9	2848	344*	94.93	9	15	30	270.3	49	767	23	33.34
West Indies		71	117	13	6627	270	63.72	23	26	45	359.2	58	1038	27	38.44
Comm. XI		3	4		243	98	60.75		3	1					
Combined J/BG XI		1	2		51	30	25.50								
L. Parkinson's XI		1	2		152	134	76.00	1			8	0	37	1	37.00
TEST RECORD		22	40	4	2190	270*	60.83	10	5	14	65	7	230	0	
CAREER		103	164	22	9921	344*	69.86	33	44	76	635.5	107	1842	51	36.11

West Indies: Test record against each team

Opponents	M	I	No	Runs	H.S.	Avge	100	50	CT	OV	MD	Runs	W
					BATTING						**BOWLING**		
England	16	29	3	1852	270*	71.23	8	5	13	62	7	212	0
Australia	5	10	1	336	105	37.33	2	0	1				
India	1	.1		2	2	2.00	0	0	0	3	0	18	0

Test record

Season	Opponents	M	I	No	Runs	H.S.	Avge	100	50	CT	OV	MD	Runs	W
						BATTING						**BOWLING**		
1929-30	England	4	8		703	223	87.87	4		4	23	2	77	0
1930-31	Australia	5	10	1	336	105	37.33	2		1				
1933	England	3	6	1	277	169*	55.40	1	1	4	19	1	81	0
1934-35	England	4	6	1	485	270*	97.00	1	2	4	5	3	3	0
1939	England	3	5		334	107	66.80	2	2		4	0	17	0
1947-48	England	1	2	1	36	29	36.00				6	1	11	0
1948-49	India	1	1		2	2	2.00				3	0	18	0
1953-54	England	1	2		17	16	8.50			1	5	0	23	0

Test record at each venue

Venue	M	I	No	Runs	H.S.	Avge	100	50	CT	OV	MD	Runs	W
					BATTING						**BOWLING**		
West Indies (10)													
Kensington Oval	3	6	1	267	176	53.40	1			11	1	27	0
Queens Park Oval	2	4		165	93	41.25		1	5	15	4	33	0
Bourda	2	3		279	114	93.00	2	1	2	3	1	8	0
Sabina Park	3	5	1	520	270*	130.00	2		2	10	0	46	0
Australia (5)													
Adelaide Oval	1	2		11	11	5.50							
Sydney Cricket Ground	2	4		151	105	37.75	1						
Brisbane	1	2	1	130	102*	130.00	1						
Melbourne Cricket Ground	1	2		44	33	22.00							
England (6)													
Lord's	2	4		276	107	69.00	2	1	1				
Old Trafford	2	4	1	249	169*	83.00	1	1	1	15	1	65	0
The Oval	2	3		86	65	28.66		1	2	8	0	33	0
India (1)													
Delhi	1	1		2	2	2.00			1	3	0	18	0

Hundred partnerships in Tests

Second wicket

227	R.K. Nunes 92, Headley 223	v England at Sabina Park	1929-30
	(Record v England until Rowe & Kallicharran 249 in 1973-74)		
	(Overall record until Sobers & Hunte 446 v Pakistan in 1957-58)		
200	I. Barrow 105, Headley 169*	v England at Old Trafford	1933
192	C.A. Roach 77, Headley 114	v England at Bourda	1929-30
156	C.A. Roach 77, Headley 176	v England at Kensington Oval	1929-30
152	F.R. Martin 123*, Headley 105	v Australia at Sydney	1930-31
	(Record v Australia until Hunte & Kanhai 163 in 1960-61)		
118	J.B. Stollmeyer 59, Headley 106	v England at Lord's	1939
113	J.B. Stollmeyer 59, Headley 65	v England at The Oval	1939

Third wicket

202	J.E.D. Sealy 91, Headley 270*	v England at Sabina Park	1934-35
	(Overall record v England until Weekes & Worrell 338 in 1953-54)		
142	F.I. de Caires 70, Headley 176	v England at Bridgetown	1929-30
110	G.C. Grant 62, Headley 105	v Australia at Sydney	1930-31
	(Record v Australia until Walcott & Weekes 127 in 1954-55)		

Seventh wicket

147	R.S. Grant 62, Headley 270*	v England at Sabina Park	1934-35
	(Record v England until Smith & Goddard 154 in 1957)		
	(Overall record until Atkinson & Depeiza 347 v Australia 1954-55)		

Test centuries in each innings (2)

114 & 112	v England 3rd Test at Bourda	1929-30
106 & 107	v England 1st Test at Lord's	1939

Test double centuries (2)

223	v England 4th Test at Sabina Park	1929-30
270*	v England 4th Test at Sabina Park	1934-35

First class record: Jamaica against each team

Opponents	M	I	No	Runs	H.S.	Avge	100	50	CT	OV	MD	Runs	W	Avge
				BATTING								**BOWLING**		
L.H. Tennyson's XI	6	9	2	1132	344*	161.71	4	3	4	18	3	56	2	28.00
Julien Cahn's XI	2	4		139	57	34.75		1	6	21	3	73	1	73.00
M.C.C. Tourists	7	10	2	499	127	62.37	1	5	7	26.3	4	81	1	81.00
Yorkshire Tourists	3	5		266	118	53.20	1	2	3	44	9	91	1	91.00
Trinidad	4	4	1	330	160	110.00	1	2	6	43	8	137	8	17.12
Barbados	2	3	3	339	203*			1	2	2	43	12	102	5	20.40
British Guiana	2	2	1	40	36	40.00			2	75	10	227	5	45.40
West Indies	1	1		103	103	103.00	1							

Record: Best bowling

Jamaica v Trinidad   26th, 27th 28th June 1946   8-2-33-5

Types of dismissals

	1st Class	Test
Caught	70	18
LBW	32	4
Bowled	17	7
Run out	9	3
Stumped	8	3
Hit wicket	6	1
Not out	21	4
Retired hurt	1	0
Totals	164	40

Over 1,000 runs in a season

Season	Opponents	Runs	Avge	100's
1933	v England	2320	66.28	7
1939	v England	1745	72.70	6
1930-31	v Australia	1066	44.41	4

'Ducks'

Headley was only ever out for three scores of '0'

Dec 1930   West Indies v Australia

Jan 1935   West Indies v England

Aug 1939   West Indies v Somerset

Record partnerships

World record 6th wicket in 1932 at Melbourne Park 487* with C.C. Passailaigue

Jamaican record 3rd wicket in 1932 at Melbourne Park 248 with I. Barrow

Bowlers who have dismissed Headley on most occasions

7 Verity, 4 Ironmonger, 3 Grimmett, 3 Allom, 3, O'Connor, 3, Paine, 3 Copson

Headley was dismissed in both innings of a game on 50 occasions, 12 of which were by the same bowler.

First class record: Teams played against on tour with West Indies

Opponents	M	I	No	Runs	H.S.	Avge	100	50	CT	OV	MD	Runs	W	Avge
Lancashire	4	7	2	288	76*	57.60		2	1	20.4	4	68	3	22.66
Glamorgan	3	4		257	129	64.25	1	1	2	29.4	4	87	2	43.50
Northamptonshire	2	3		120	63	40.00		2	3	3	1	9	1	9.00
Essex	2	4	2	226	116*	113.00	1	1	1	10	2	31	1	31.00
Somerset	2	3	1	255	224*	127.50	1		3	20	4	56	1	56.00
Middlesex	2	3		286	227	95.33	1		1	28	4	74	5	14.80
Derbyshire	2	3	1	296	200*	148.00	1	1		13	6	21	1	21.00
Yorkshire	2	4	1	131	61	43.66		1	2	9	1	16	0	
Nottinghamshire	2	2	1	300	234*	300.00	1	1	2	11	1	42	0	
Surrey	2	3		145	93	48.33		2	2					
Leicestershire	1	2		71	60	35.50		1		4	2	14	0	
Warwickshire	1	1		182	182	182.00	1			6	0	17	0	
Kent	1	2		62	38	31.00			1	6	0	33	0	
Sussex	1	2		110	79	55.00		1	1	3	1	10	0	
Worcestershire	1	2		57	50	28.50		1		1	1	0	0	
Hampshire	1	1		6	6	6.00								
Gloucestershire	1	2		45	40	22.50				1	0	1	0	
M.C.C.	2	2		149	129	74.50	1		1	4	0	12	1	12.00
Cambridge University	2	2		178	103	89.00	1	1		5	0	20	1	20.00
Oxford University	1	2		74	56	37.00		1	1	27	3	77	3	25.66
England XI	1	1		167	167	167.00	1		1	5	0	19	3	6.33
H.D.G. Leveson-Gower's XI	1	2		49	35	24.50			1	11	2	46	0	
New South Wales	2	4		179	82	44.75		2	2					
Victoria	2	4		355	131	88.75	2	1	1	4	0	24	0	
South Australia	2	4		157	75	39.25		1		2	0	12	0	
Queensland	1	2		36	19	18.00			2	1	0	3	0	
Tasmania	1	1		3	3	3.00			1					
Holkar State	1	1		1	1	1.00				2	2	0	0	
North Zone	1	1		8	8	8.00			1	46	2	95	3	31.66
Pakistan	1	1	1	57	57*			1	1	20	11	21	2	10.50

Record in 'League' cricket

Year	M	Runs	H.S.	Avge	100	50	Runs	W	Avge
			BATTING				**BOWLING**		
Haslingden (Lancashire League									
1934	25	1063	162*	50.62	3	4	979	59	16.59
1935	23	917	82	61.13		10	776	34	22.82
1936	22	940	128*	58.75	1	6	786	54	14.55
1937	23	1360	122*	97.15	5	7	736	41	17.96
1938	23	677	91	37.61		6	737	76	9.70
Haslingden (Worsley Cup)									
1938	8	364	189	45.50	1	1	393	21	18.71
Haslingden (League play-offs)									
1938	3	189	79	63.00		3	107	0	
Bacup (Lancashire League)									
1950	20	747	109*	57.46	2	5	438	13	33.69
Bacup (Worsley Cup)									
1950	2	162	145*	162.00	1		85	7	12.14
Dudley (Birmingham League)									
1951	17	922	111	76.83	1	9	533	36	14.81
1952	15	727	169*	72.70	3	3	269	21	12.81
1953	17	765	141	76.50	3	2	370	29	12.76
1954	12	464	95*	66.28		4	258	16	16.13
Totals									
Haslingden	127	5510	189		10	37	4514	285	15.83
Bacup	22	909	145*		3	5	523	20	26.15
Dudley	61	2878	169*		7	18	1430	102	14.01
Career	**210**	**9298**	**189**		**20**	**60**	**6467**	**407**	**15.88**